D0996284

Gardening in Pyjamas

HELEN YEMM

Gardening in Pyjamas

HORTICULTURAL ENLIGHTENMENT FOR OBSESSIVE DAWN RAIDERS

SIMON &
SCHUSTER
ILLUSTRATED

London · New York · Sydney · Toronto · New Delhi

A CBS COMPANY

First published in Great Britain in 2013 by Simon & Schuster UK Ltd
A CBS COMPANY

Previously published as *Gardening in Your Nightie* (2000)

1 3 5 7 9 10 8 6 4 2

SIMON & SCHUSTER ILLUSTRATED BOOKS
Simon & Schuster UK Ltd
222 Gray's Inn Road
London
WC1X 8HB

www.simonandschuster.co.uk

Simon & Schuster Australia, Sydney

Simon & Schuster India, New Delhi

A CIP catalogue record for this book is available
from the British Library

ISBN: 978-1-47112-658-1

Illustrations by Francine Lawrence
Designed and typeset by Richard Proctor
Edited by Sharon Amos
Printed and bound in Great Britain by
CPI Group (UK) Ltd, Croydon, CR0 4YY

DEDICATION

This book is dedicated to the memory of my mother, Marie Yemm, the original Nightie Gardener. It was also written with my son Henry very much in mind, in the hope that he will one day acquire a garden, a trowel and the obligatory items of clothing – and discover that he is destined to become yet another chip off the old block.

ACKNOWLEDGEMENTS

I should like to thank all my fellow gardeners who have kept on telling me over the past decade that *Gardening in Your Nightie* really hit the spot. It was they who sowed the seeds that grew into this new, updated and improved version: *Gardening in Pyjamas*. I am grateful, too, to MWN for suggesting that I should stop talking, stop messing around in the garden, and just get on with it.

I am again indebted to my editor, Sharon Amos, who waved her magic wand over the *Thorny Problems* book and has done so again with this one. Last but not least, thanks to Lorraine Jerram and the team at Simon & Schuster for their support and enthusiasm, and indeed to their former Editorial Director, Francine Lawrence, for the lovely drawings that are sprinkled around the book.

Contents

Wise words from an (alas) anonymous
pyjamas gardener...

'I've come to the conclusion that, with gardening,
if you can manage to put it off for long enough,
eventually it's too late.'

So, what do *you* wear when you're gardening?

Some years ago, during a lull in the cut-and-thrust, question-and-answer part of one of the gardening classes I used to give, some bright spark, no doubt feeling the need to show keenness by volunteering a question, asked *'What do you wear when you are gardening?'* I always assured my nervous novices that no question would be too daft, so I was obliged to answer this one in all seriousness: *'My nightie, as often as not – and wet slippers.'*

Thus was born the title of my first book (written in 2000) *Gardening in Your Nightie*. It was based on the kind of basic stuff I used to teach and written very much from the heart for fellow gardeners – women – for it is they who seemed to do most of the obsessive horticultural grovelling and grafting and apparently still do. Despite being an un-glamorous, un-illustrated paperback (*definitely* no pictures of the author *en chemise de nuit*) – *Nightie* nevertheless hit the spot for, among others, the then gardening editor of *The Daily Telegraph*. It led ultimately to more than a decade of garden writing, most notably my weekly no-nonsense 'Thorny Problems' letters page in the *Telegraph*'s Saturday gardening supplement, condensed into a book of the same name in 2011.

In the years since I first put fingertips to clunky word processor, much has changed. Accusations of mild sexism, twenty-first-century wardrobe refinements and general horticultural correctness necessitated the title change to *Gardening in Pyjamas* for this updated version. But more seriously, the use of chemicals in the garden has changed radically in a more ecologically conscious world, providing us with unavoidable challenges, while the word organic – even when used with a very small 'o' – has to be more keenly acknowledged than heretofore. An extra decade of experience has changed the horticultural habits even of old diehards like me.

It would appear, however, that avid gardeners are still up to the same old tricks. Out they go in the early hours full of good intentions, as often as not with a battered fleece flung on over inadequate nightwear and with a long-gone-cold cup of instant clutched in hand. They plan, plot and dream, interrupting their reverie to tweak here, poke there, even hitching things up a bit to facilitate a plunge into the back of a border to nip off an errant shoot perhaps, or to tweak at a weed. For the lucky home-based few, these shenanigans can go on for the best part of a morning, cut short only by the arrival of a bemused visitor at the front door. For most, however, early-morning raids may constitute the principal gardening time in the week. A glance at a scratched watch face has them scurrying indoors, scrubbing the soil from knees and fingernails, throwing on more respectable garments and rushing to work, leaving the sartorial secrets of their muddy habit strewn damply over the unmade bed.

Real gardening basics have not changed that much, however, and it occurred to me that now that the infamous gung-ho-paint-it-all-blue instant makeover years have thankfully faded into history, the unglamorous facts of life (or death) out there that can so thoroughly befuddle beginners, need spelling out and explaining again in words of (mostly) one syllable. So *Gardening in Pyjamas* aims again to cater for those new (and not so new) to gardening who have lots of questions they scarcely dare ask – but want the answers to be kept simple. It is for those who want to know how to achieve a beautiful garden, but have been scratching about indecisively using inappropriate tools, with sodden hair and a wrecked back, wondering all the while whether actually they have been doing more harm than good. Deep down in their aching bones they know that gardening could be the ultimate leisure pleasure if only they understood just a little bit more about it.

The *Thorny Problems* book seems to have found its way to many a bedside table (or – yes, I know – the bookshelf in the loo), and I fervently hope that *Gardening in Pyjamas* does the same. There are still, as you will have noticed on your first perfunctory flip-through, no mouth-watering illustrations to bring on irrational shopping trips, no tedious photographic step-by-steps featuring a model with immaculate fingernails and not a single demoralising line drawing showing you how to prune improbably perfect shrubs. I learnt a lot of my gardening by just getting stuck in and having a go, armed with some helpful basic information gleaned largely from my parents, both of them botanists, teachers and skilful gardeners. What follows is my version of that information augmented by my own experience and it will, I hope, make your precious gardening time more rewarding. I hope you will dip in when desperate and find just enough to get you started, but not enough to scare you stiff.

CHAPTER 1

What a lot of gardeners don't know and don't like to ask

As I write, there are scores of perfectly competent gardeners scratching away in their beloved oases as happy as sandboys, but for that occasional, irritating thought that there is a whole lot of stuff about plants that they just don't know – and that might have made their horticultural lives a little easier. I am not talking about advanced botany, or serious science, but the basic things that many gardening books and experienced gardening friends take for granted that we know – the lack of real understanding of which can eat away at our self-confidence and consequently get in the way of imaginative and satisfying gardening.

It is all a bit like those early school experiences that dog you for the rest of your life. I think I was 'away' the first time my class encountered long division. I never ever got the hang of it, and I have never ever dared ask anyone to explain it to me since. My subsequent terror of maths, I am convinced, stems from that time. Thank God for the invention of calculators.

If you walk round a garden with its really learned owners, they will explain everything and anything to you, for most love to talk. But you are hardly likely to stop them in mid-flow to ask them what they mean when they say such-and-such is a useful biennial. Most probably you won't get to ask the really meaty questions that are burning within, for fear of revealing scores of gaps in your basic knowledge and looking silly. Furthermore, gardeners are hopelessly generous and in return for your appreciation will invariably press trowelfuls of their treasures or, even worse, branches of rare shrubs for you to 'take a few cuttings' from, all of them with incomprehensible Latin names, on to you. It is all supposed to be part of the fun, a tangible expression of the overwhelming need

1

of most gardeners to share their enthusiasm with others. But it can be equally overwhelming to be on the receiving end. So here is my guide to that common language we gardeners use to communicate.

REAL BASICS YOU NEED TO GRASP

I should hate this book to become one of those useful but dry little numbers – an A to Z of largely obscure horticultural terms. You sense that the writer of such books has been dredging around trying to fill each letter section with as many definitions as he or she can find to make you realise how much there is you don't know about plants and gardening. I will try to include explanations of key words within each section of the book, but I do think it is important to understand exactly what the following mean before you read on.

Annuals

An annual plant is one that completes its growing cycle during one season and will not survive frost. This group of plants includes petunias, busy Lizzies, nasturtiums and so on, and most of them need a lot of sun.

The term hardy annual applies to those plants whose seeds can be sown directly into the ground in spring or even autumn. Their seeds germinate as soon as the soil is warm enough and the days long enough – they then cope with whatever Mother Nature throws at them. Many hardy annuals will therefore self-seed, so that once you introduce plants such as love-in-the-mist, marigolds or nasturtiums into your garden, you will find that they become a more or less permanent fixture, which is quite fun.

Most annuals, however, are tender and have to be raised from seed in a warm greenhouse or on a windowsill indoors. Being expensive to buy and time-consuming to maintain, they should be grown in pots and other containers, and used to create bright spots of colour or fill gaps in a new garden. My real favourites are the big annuals: cosmos, cleome and tobacco plants. You have to make sure you get hold of *Nicotiana affinis* if you want those big, white tobacco plants that glow in the dark and knock you sideways with their scent. (I have actually known garden centre staff to fib about what they offer you. Many of the modern cultivars available are miserable little scentless things, I find.) These larger annuals, real floppy whoppers, spend the midsummer months achieving their often breathtaking height, and then reward you with flowers well into the early autumn, when the rest of the average British garden can look a bit sad and burnt out.

At the end of autumn, pull out exhausted annuals and chuck them away, even though they may look as though they want to jolly on past Christmas. You can keep some seed of the best of them, and start again the following year.

Biennials

A biennial plant is one that takes two growing seasons to complete its cycle. During the first year the new seedlings produce a small amount of rather uninteresting leaf growth but do not flower. If they survive the ravages of slugs, snails and fanatical weeders until the next year, they will produce loads of flowers, millions of seeds and die a very ugly and dramatic death at the end of the summer. The most well-known examples are foxgloves, honesty and forget-me-nots. It is really important to learn to identify biennials when they are very young – you can do this by comparing the leaves of the baby and the adult – because you can quite easily transplant biennials after their first year of growth. Indeed it is generally necessary to thin the seedlings out where they make colonies and threaten to stunt each other's growth. I adore the self-seeding biennial population of my garden – constantly ebbing and flowing, providing bits of haphazard colour in unexpected places. If it threatens to overwhelm, I just weed things out.

There is a variation to biennials. Some plants, notably angelica and some verbascums, are what is known as monocarpic, which means they may take more than two years to become mature enough to flower and set seed, after which they generally die.

Perennials

A perennial (also referred to as a herbaceous perennial) is a frost-hardy, non-woody plant (in other words not a shrub, see below) that comes up year after year. In this group are the favourite summer flowerers – lupins, delphiniums, campanulas and so on. As I explain in the chapter on mixed borders (see pages 81–112), perennials do need a certain amount of attention – protection from slugs, annual feeding, supporting with canes or twigs, deadheading to keep them flowering for as long as possible, cutting down to ground level in the winter and division every few years – but they are incredibly rewarding once established. A few, generally short-lived perennials (such as the Welsh poppy and sweet rocket) will seed themselves gently around the garden. I love that, and it is one of the main reasons it is so important to learn to distinguish seedlings from weedlings.

Half-hardy perennials
These include many fuchsias, argyranthemums (marguerites), pelargoniums (geraniums), verbenas and helichrysums, which are mostly used for container planting. These plants are true perennials in their

native (hotter) climates, and can limp though most mild winters in towns (where it is a degree or so warmer), if they are given the shelter of a wall, kept fairly dry, and if their roots remain unfrosted. Even if you overwinter them in a greenhouse or porch, where they may be subjected to bad pest attacks, they have to be cut back, cleaned up and generally 'rejuvenated' in the late spring if they are to perform well the following year.

Shrubs and trees

A shrub or bush is a plant with several woody stems coming from the base and can be anything from 15cm (6in) to 6m (20ft) in height. Those sold in UK garden centres and nurseries should all be frost hardy, although ideas about 'climate change' have brought a rush of blood to the head to some nurserymen and I have on occasion seen tender shrubs such as some abutilons and *Lantana camara* sold without a warning label to say they wouldn't stand frost. Some hardy shrubs may suffer winter damage to their extremities if they are exposed to icy winds but will generally recover the following summer. Almost all shrubs need pruning or tidying at some point during the year once they are established.

A tree is a single-stemmed woody plant from a few feet to well over 15m (50ft) in height. Some trees (notably eucalyptus, paulownia and some willows) can be persuaded to become almost shrub-like by being stooled each year in the spring – that is, cut right to the ground and encouraged to make several branches from their bases.

THE NAMING OF PLANTS

It was not until I started gardening that I really discovered the value of Latin. More than anything, Latin plant names seem to fill people with horror. The fact that we no longer study Latin in most of our schools seems a huge shame. Initially I hated the subject as much as most, but began to realise fairly early on that Latin not only held the key to English spelling but also helped to lessen one's fear of learning other European languages. After an otherwise hopelessly flawed school career

– I think I could best be described as detention-seeking – my Latin has become a welcome reminder that I am not without a brain. All those jars of broad beans that mouldered away on the school lab windowsill when everyone else's flourished, all that stuff about amoeba and spirogyra, the life cycle of the tapeworm, and questions on the natural vegetation of the tundra – freesias, was my oh-so-bright response, I recall – went in one ear and out of the other. But my familiarity with Latin has really helped me with plant names.

The binomial system of naming plants, as it is called, dates back to the eighteenth century, when a Swedish botanist, Carl Linnaeus, decided that all plants should be given Latinised names (actually many of the generic names come from Greek) consisting of two words: the name of the genus (see below) – e.g. *Potentilla, Skimmia, Delphinium* or whatever – and the name of the species (see below) – e.g. *fruticosa, nepalensis, japonica, alba, neumanniana,* or some such. Thus the 'surname' comes first, and the 'first name' comes second. Heaven only knows what kind of chap Linnaeus was, and can you imagine what kind of gardener he must have been? I bet poor old Mrs Linnaeus (*Linnaeus mrs kitchenensis*, perhaps?) had a hard job stopping him planting things in rows and putting labels on everything.

The reason why we are stuck with an embellished form of this ancient system is because it really is necessary. We simply cannot get by with common 'English' names because they don't describe the plant accurately. I use common names whenever I can do so without causing confusion: how can we abandon such evocative gems as lady's mantle, love-in-the-mist, granny's bonnet, love-lies-bleeding, Solomon's seal, lily-of-the-valley and many more? So, like many gardeners, I use a confusing jumble of names, a compromise, in rather the same way that I have managed partially to convert to metric measurements: I am more than capable of saying that such-and-such is 3 feet high and 30 centimetres wide (and most people of my generation don't bat an eyelid). But we do need to take it all on board. I will therefore try to give a broad outline of how the system works as simply as I can, while apologising to real botanists for probably oversimplifying the whole issue.

I shall use the following plants to illustrate my description: *Potentilla fruticosa* var. *arbuscula*, *Potentilla fruticosa* 'Elizabeth' and *Potentilla nepalensis* 'Miss Willmott'. I have chosen potentilla as an example since I know that it causes confusion. Why, I have been asked by more than one disappointed novice, is it that the sad little sprawly potentilla they put in their own garden bears so little resemblance to the familiar shrubby pale-yellow-flowered one resplendent all summer long in their friend's garden? This is my rather long-winded reply. Bear with me.

Plant families

All plants belong in 'families', the members of which share certain botanical characteristics that may or may not be obvious to gardeners. If you look closely at the individual flowers of sweet peas, laburnum and clover, for example, you will see they are similar in shape. They all belong to the pea family (*Leguminaceae*). If you visit a botanic garden, you will find plants grown in large beds with other members of their family. It is quite a good way of putting the jigsaw puzzle together, but actually the family names are, I think, the least important part of a plant's name, from our point of view.

The genus

Plant families are broken down further into smaller groups or genera (the singular of which is genus), containing plants that are even more closely related. But the genus *Potentilla* (which belongs, incidentally, to the rose family, *Rosaceae*), contains both shrubs and herbaceous perennials (see pages 4–5), which, though they have similar flowers, for example, have different growing habits or other subtle characteristics. This is why the name potentilla (or cinquefoil, its common name, which is a corruption of French) on its own is pretty unhelpful, particularly when you are out shopping.

Plant species

The vital second word on a plant label, or in a plant directory, is the species name. This will often, but by no means always, tell you a lot about the plant. It will describe either how it looks or smells, tell you where it comes from or even tell you the name of the person who first found it growing in the wild and brought it into cultivation. This is generally the part of the plant name that gives new gardeners the collywobbles, but it is not too hard to learn a few of the more obvious ones (which are related to English words), and find a book that tells you the meaning of the more obscure-sounding ones. For example, *Potentilla fruticosa* is a shrubby or woody (which is what *'fruticosa'* means) plant; *Potentilla nepalensis* (from Nepal) happens to be an herbaceous or non-woody one. Even if you do not have the energy to get to grips with the actual meaning of each one, you really need to know that this part of the name is important.

Varieties

I am afraid there is more, much more. There is generally a third word (sometimes Latinised, sometimes English) on the plant label. This is the variety name – a further category that helps to identify plants more precisely. If it is a naturally occurring variation in a plant, say a different leaf or flower coloration, then it will be quite simple – *variegata* (variegated), *alba* (white), *hirsutum* (hairy) and so on. Hence *Potentilla fruticosa* var. *arbuscula* (meaning something like 'shrubby little bush'). If it is a cultivated variety (i.e. a variation that has occurred since it

8

became a garden plant), then it will often have a recognisable English or other European language name written within quotes. Thus *Potentilla fruticosa* 'Elizabeth', or *Potentilla nepalensis* 'Miss Willmott'. The term cultivated variety is now often shortened to 'cultivar'.

How knowing the Latin name can help you buy the right plant

In fact using the diversity of the potentilla tribe mentioned above helps illustrate this rather neatly. How did those nervous novices get it so wrong? The explanation is usually simple: they remembered the name 'potentilla', swanned off to the garden centre and grabbed the first potentilla they came across. Their friends may have *Potentilla fruticosa* 'Primrose Beauty' or 'Elizabeth' growing in their gardens – both easy-to-grow bushy shrubs. What the novices acquired by mistake was *Potentilla nepalensis* 'Miss Willmott', perhaps, or 'Gibson's Scarlet', popular cultivars of an herbaceous species of the same genus – got that? – that die right back in winter. It's the perfect illustration of why you really do need to go beyond the generic name and get quite specific, to be sure of buying the right plant.

Hybrids

And then there are hybrids, which occur when two species from the same genera are deliberately crossed. If you see multiplication signs in the middle of plant names, this indicates a hybrid; for example, *Primula × bulleesiana* is a hybrid between *Primula beesiana* and *Primula bulleyana*... This is the point at which most of us glaze over and switch on the telly for light relief, so I will draw a veil over the rest. Suffice it to say that F1 hybrids are hybrids with attitude – plants with greater vigour, better flowers and often greater disease resistance. More than that the average gardener really, really does not need to know.

While on the subject of hybrids, I have a few pet hates. The introduction of so many new garden plant varieties and hybrids is, in my view, a sign that horticulture has gone mad. I suppose I can understand the reason for breeding plants to promote improved disease resistance, more intense scent and, perhaps, even bigger and better flowers, all of which matter to a lot of gardeners. However, I am sure I am not alone in looking sideways at some of those awful recent additions – lurid pansies and petunias, variegated spirea, ceanothus and cistus, which I think look either sick or totally alien or both.

Changing names

Another pet hate is the way botanists periodically get into huddles and change plant names, presumably when they think we gardeners are getting a bit too cocky. How many young(ish) gardeners have parents who still insist on calling *Philadelphus* (commonly known as mock orange), *Syringa*, when everyone under the age of 50 knows *Syringa* is now the Latin name for lilac? And did you know that ubiquitous ever-grey shrub with those love 'em or hate 'em yellow ragwort flowers is no longer called *Senecio*, but is now *Brachyglottis*? I suppose we should be grateful as we never could make up our minds whether to pronounce it SeNEKio or SenEESio. But the new name sounds like a nasty throat infection however you say it.

And that non-invasive weeping bamboo *Arundinaria murielae* is now called *Fargesia murielae*, while the lovely, easy, early-flowering perennial *Dicentra spectabilis* (aka bleeding heart) has recently been renamed *Lamprocapnos spectabilis*. Trying to keep up with it all makes me feel very weary, it really does.

Pronunciation

Which brings me to pronunciation. Many obsessed gardeners spend a lot of time thumbing through books and mumbling darkly to themselves, thankful that they are not having to read out loud. If you care about 'accepted' pronunciation, you can get one of those books on plant names that will give you their phonetic pronunciation. If you don't, then just keep your ears open and you will be amazed at what you hear coming out of the mouths of even those whom you might think should know. Once when I was appearing on the same television programme as Peter Seabrook (the Godfather of telly gardening), we each pronounced the name *Lysimachia punctata* totally differently, bold as brass, for all to hear. And guess what? The world did not come to an end.

Incidentally, I have noticed that whenever a few friendly gardeners get together they invariably have a good laugh about mutual mispronunciations. The name *Cotoneaster* springs to mind. I think most of us started off as members of the Cotton Easter club. As I say, who cares?

Returning briefly and absolutely finally to the subject of the necessity for Latin names, there is now a more pressing reason to persevere with them. If you happen, as I do, to start 'oohing' and 'aahing' about plants in nurseries in foreign parts, you can 'ooh' and 'aah' together with foreign gardeners *in Latin*. (I just love to hear Italians speak Latin. I suspect that even their words for well-rotted horse manure sound like the finer parts of a Catholic Mass.) There is no doubt about it, using Latin plant names does make you feel like a real gardener and very grown-up. And while you might have an almighty job finding something as simple as a bag of bonemeal in a French garden centre, I find that buying plants there is, comparatively speaking, a doddle.

Once you have all of the above under your belt, you may read on...

CHAPTER 2

The good earth

How on earth, I have been asking myself, do you make a chapter on soil in a gardening book interesting? Well, I have to try.

Considering how much time we spend grubbing about in it, scraping it out from under our fingernails and sweeping clods of it off the kitchen floor, it is amazing how little we really understand about soil. Things are looking up, however. Twenty years or so ago, as often as not we did nothing to our garden soil apart from sprinkle a bit of peat on it from time to time or empty out old growbags, or the compost from old house-plant casualties, on to the flower beds. (I know a dear old thing who for years has given her strapping 6-foot camellia three old tea bags a day: on reflection, maybe she was on to something – perhaps that is how it got to be strapping in the first place.) Nowadays, however, it has become second nature to even the most innocent of gardeners to bandy about words like 'mulch', 'compost' and the need for 'soil improvement'. Even the slackest among us feels a twinge of unease if, pressed for time, we just scrape a hole in a piece of the compacted, dry, urban filth that passes for soil, bung a plant in it and splosh a bit of water about, hoping for the best.

TOPSOIL

There is a lot of science behind it all, of course, but it is relatively easy stuff. Plants need to grow in good topsoil – that is, a mixture of ground-up rock particles that contain a variety of vital minerals, plus water, air, and decayed animal and vegetable matter that eventually forms humus, vital to plant growth, as well as bacteria and micro-organisms, which form natural nutrients. Plants thrive in soil that has balanced proportions of the so-called macronutrients: nitrogen, phosphorus and potassium (described as N, P and K on fertiliser packets – more on these later).

Beneath the topsoil is subsoil, which cannot support plant life. It is mostly a mixture of rock particles, minerals and water, plus – for many of us – bricks and broken tiles, bits of old bike, scraps of smashed china and general domestic detritus. I have become convinced, over many years of digging in various gardens, that an ancient English tribal rite consisted of going out of the back door and throwing crockery around. So great is the volume of the stuff I have dug up in my time that I am sure I could reassemble several tea services.

Depending on where you live, your topsoil can be anything from a few centimetres to about 50cm (20in) deep, and it can be acid or alkaline. Soil over limestone or chalk is alkaline; soil over ancient woodland or marshland is generally acid. The soil pH – its level of alkalinity or acidity – can be quite easily assessed, to work out which plants will grow well.

To further complicate matters, soil particle size dramatically affects the texture of the soil, which is also deeply significant to gardeners. Soil can be clay-based, with small particles, which ensure that it either bakes hard, almost with a crust on it, or becomes waterlogged. While it is often extremely fertile, soil like this is difficult for plant roots to penetrate and compacts easily if walked on when it is wet. It is generally referred to as feeling 'sticky', but I prefer to call it 'slithery' to the touch. It is extremely hard to dig except at certain times of year, when it is neither too wet nor too dry. Then there is sand-based, silty soil that you can almost run through your fingers when it is dry. It consists of coarse particles and tends to drain too quickly so that nutrients wash through it and it easily becomes infertile. Few of us have what every gardener covets: good loam, which has equal proportions of sand, clay and the organic matter that breaks down to form humus.

Problems

Whatever its basic type, topsoil in most small gardens suffers from one or other of the following two problems.

Unless it has been regularly 'topped up' with organic matter, it is thin, dusty and infertile, having been over-cultivated for generations. Since the demise of the horse as an easy-to-come-by source of coarse, texture-improving, nitrogen-rich manure, things have gone from bad to worse. Access to the average back garden can be difficult, so even if you have a convenient source, carrying bags of muck or other goodies through the house is not a joyful task. But with little or no input of meaningful organic matter, our garden soil is just not giving of its best.

The other frequent problem that arises where builders have been active is that areas of topsoil may have been unwittingly polluted or, worse, churned up completely so that what passes for topsoil is actually subsoil, with little or no nutrients or humus in it, at all. Unless instructed to do so, builders rarely do the sensible gardening thing and, before digging foundations for walls, excavating drains or whatever, reserve in a special pile the topsoil they removed so that order (and gardening) can be returned swiftly to the site once they have departed.

Solutions

While not wishing to oversimplify a very complex subject, I cannot stress enough that both of these frequently encountered soil problems can be largely overcome if you regularly fork loads of coarse organic matter into garden soil around plants. (In this sense, the word organic means that the matter was once living.) You should also incorporate organic stuff into the soil by trench digging (see pages 91–2) where possible, before planting up new beds and borders. What you add to the soil is up to you, and you should have at least a vague idea of your soil pH (see page 23) when you make that choice.

For me, home-made compost is the best organic stuff, but few gardens can generate enough. When I run out of home-made, I use spent mushroom compost (from the mushroom-growing industry), or recycled composted council waste, both of which are easy to come by and don't smell awful. In some areas, there are still people who sell mushroom compost from the back of a lorry and will bag it up for you. It is slightly alkaline (see page 23) and not as nutritious as nitrogen-rich recycled waste or (if you can get it) thoroughly rotted horse manure.

I generally top up my soil fertility each spring with blood, fish and bone or with pelleted chicken manure: organic-based fertilisers bought in bags from garden centres. These are balanced fertilisers with roughly equal proportions of N, P and K. If you, like me, have clay soil – you will know because it will be so hard to dig when it is very dry or very wet – I find it is helpful to add coarse sand or grit along with the organic matter as part of the soil preparation process. This will make it much easier to deal with, opening up the texture so that it drains more efficiently. Sandy soil that drains too freely is also improved by the regular addition of enormous quantities of organic matter.

As I see it, the key is to concentrate on improving soil texture. Then, whatever nutrients you add in the form of fertilisers, whether they are organic or inorganic balanced fertilisers, time-release capsules or the convenient quick-acting soluble kinds (detailed later), will be retained together with moisture and air. The whole root-growing environment is thus transformed.

So much for the basics. I feel it would be useful to look at some aspects of the whole subject in greater detail. Along the way we should get to understand a little more about what is meant by such things as soil fertility and fertilisers generally, compost (there's a confusing word for a start), trench digging, mulching and the much-misunderstood question of soil pH.

SOIL FERTILITY

As I have previously mentioned, plants need the so-called macronutrients – nitrogen, phosphorus and potassium – to grow and flower well. They also need trace elements, such as magnesium, boron and copper, but... enough science for one page. You just have to think of plants as children – needing a good diet in order to grow.

Plants show various symptoms when grown in infertile soil – their leaves are paler, their flowers fewer and their growth less vigorous than their well-nourished friends. Research has apparently shown that adding fertilisers to our gardens does not have as much effect as we would hope. I can only tell you about my first garden, which belonged to a tall house in West London. Heavily under the influence of my parents, both keen gardeners and botanists, I was dragooned into applying masses of rotted horse manure to my whole garden before they would let me plant so much as a single wallflower. As I recall we carried it in great bundles through the house, over the new carpet, slung in a pair of huge old curtains that my mother had sacrificed for the purpose. Such dedication to horticulture was not unusual in our household.

A year or so later, I was standing one evening at the window at the very top of the house with my small son, watching the planes (remember Concorde?) and helicopters coming in over the London rooftops. As he whooped with joy and waved a sticky index finger at an approaching helicopter, I recall vividly my amazement as I looked down at our garden. It was quite noticeable that in our plot, the greenery was two shades darker, the flowers were that much brighter, and everything was taller and juicier looking, than in any of the other gardens in the little row of similar plots below me. All that goodness in the soil was actually visible.

You can test your soil's fertility with little test-tube kits and convert your kitchen for a day into something resembling a school chemistry lab. My advice is that, unless you have a growth and health problem in certain areas of your garden, it is really not worth the effort. Whenever I have gone through the motions in various gardens I have come to the sobering conclusion that our gardens are generally likely to be equally deficient in all of the three macronutrients.

Macronutrients

Nitrogen (N) in the soil is important for leaf growth. Spring lawn treatments are therefore rich in nitrogen. However, if you give flowering plants more than they need, they will produce too much leaf and not enough flower. Nasturtiums are a good example of this. If grown in poor soil, they flower much better and produce less irritating leaf growth.

Phosphorus (P) is essential for general plant health and disease resistance. Autumn lawn food is high in phosphates – but low in nitrogen. It strengthens the grass for the winter and ensures that it has a strong start in the spring, while not encouraging it to grow fast and lush just before the cold weather.

Potassium (K), generally referred to by gardeners as 'potash', is important for the production of flowers and fruit. A 'high-potash' feed is a fertiliser that will kick-start plants into flowering. You tend to give this to flowering containers and tomatoes from about midsummer on, once you see that the plants are starting to produce their buds.

The 'O' word

Perhaps here is as good a place as any to address the word 'organic', much used and sometimes misused in horticulture. At its simplest, organic is a word applied to anything that comes originally from nature, as opposed to man-made. In the UK, the Soil Association applies the word strictly to organic gardening, and true organic gardeners use nothing man-made, setting huge store by using composts and mulches to improve soil and 'feed' plants, shunning the use of peat (see page 33), except where coir and other 'greener' innovations simply won't do the job, and, for example, using fish and bone as a general fertiliser, pelleted hop and chicken manure or products derived from seaweed as pep-up fertilisers. Treating your soil 'organically' is relatively easy and many of us (including me) have a real go at it. The problem of organic pest control is a far knottier one, which I will address in a later chapter.

General-purpose granular fertilisers

Macronutrients are traditionally applied to the garden in spring in the form of a balanced fertiliser – that is, one that has equal proportions of each element in it. During the Second World War, when efficient food production was a key factor in the national fight for survival, the government of the day developed a fertiliser – National Growmore – that has become the well-known Growmore. For years, gardeners applied the recommended 4oz per square yard around the whole garden (excluding the lawn) to give the whole shooting match a bit of a lift. Incidentally, 4oz (about 115g) is two hefty, gloved fistfuls to you and me. (You don't bother to weigh garden fertilisers the way you do sugar.)

Growmore (and now many other brands that call themselves 'balanced granular general-purpose feed' or some such catch-all name) is an inorganic fertiliser – that is, it is a man-made blend of minerals. But changing attitudes have led people to return to the traditional, organic-based 'blood, fish and bone' fertilisers – the nearest equivalent to Growmore in terms of balanced nutrients. You need less of the blood, fish and bone per square yard – approximately one fistful will do. In both cases you should fork the stuff gently into the top few centimetres of soil. The rain will do the rest. Another so-called balanced fertiliser is pelleted chicken manure, although those who market it tend to be somewhat vague about the actual N, P, K content. If you don't want to use anything containing bonemeal (and some don't like the idea) and you want to use an 'organic' fertiliser, then chicken manure may be the best answer.

If you talk to truly organic gardeners, they will tell you that if you add enough organic stuff to the soil at regular intervals, general fertilisers are not really necessary. But you can never know what 'enough' is, and I suspect it is more than ordinary gardeners have the time, patience or energy for. So I always add a general fertiliser in the spring, around March and, if I am feeling diligent, again in the middle of the summer.

Time-release fertilisers

Like general-purpose granular fertilisers, many time-release fertilisers also tend to be balanced, although some are now formulated for specific purposes (rose food, ericaceous plant food and so on, of which more on pages 21–2). They take the form of little orange capsules that you mix into the soil – or potting compost in containers – at the rate given on the packet. The capsules' silicone coating starts to dissolve and release the fertiliser within only when they are damp and the temperature is sufficiently warm for plant growth. The manufacturers claim that they are effective for a whole growing season. It seems all very clever, and is an ideal way to fertilise plants in containers and window boxes, but to me seems a bit of an extravagant way to feed a whole garden. Perhaps I am just mean and old-fashioned.

Water-in fertilisers

Soluble fertilisers are what you might call horticultural wonder drugs. There are several obviously inorganic brands (pink or blue soluble grains that look more medical than horticultural), as well as liquids that you dilute, many seaweed based, which are organic. If you want to be ultra-organic, you can even make your own high-potash feed by steeping the leaves of comfrey or nettles in a bucket of water (see opposite).

Commercially bought soluble or liquid feeds vary considerably in their N, P, K content so you should take a look at the smallest print on the packaging. What they have in common, however, is the convenience and the speed with which they take effect. The big plus about fertilisers that you water-in is that they are taken up by the roots within days and are not dependent on being washed gradually into the soil. While they are very quick to hit the spot, the effect is not as long lasting and they may need to be applied at regular intervals during the growing season – generally once a week or fortnight. There are always good instructions on the packets and bottles.

Soluble fertilisers can also be applied as a foliar feed – plants can actually take up food through their leaves – which is useful if you are short of time or during dry weather when plant roots are under stress. Spray the solution directly on to the plants' leaves. The best time to do this is early morning or evening, but never in the middle of a sunny day.

A final observation: if you ever decant fertilisers into more convenient water-proof cartons, don't forget to make a note of the dosage and any other useful instructions, and write the information on the tub (plant label marker pens do the trick), otherwise you will kick yourself. I know these things.

NETTLE OR COMFREY BREW

You will need the following:

I kg (2lb) of nettles or comfrey (Who on earth weighs nettles? Just
    cram the bucket full before adding the water)
10 litres (about 2 gallons) of water
1 bucket
1 clothes peg

The clothes peg is for your nose, since the resulting liquid smells absolutely vile.

You should dilute one part of this foul brew in ten parts of water before using it. Any that is left over at the end of the growing season should be poured, sludge and all, into your compost heap.

Specific fertilisers

There are also, as I have already mentioned, soluble, granular and time-release feeds for specific tasks or plants – roses, lawns, bedding plants, tomatoes for example – each with a different N, P, K balance, which you can see by looking at that small print on the backs of the packets. You can also buy nitrogen, potash and phosphate fertilisers separately for specific nutrient deficiencies. It can all get very complicated if you let it.

6/22240348

Bonemeal

Used traditionally in gardening as a slow-release, long-life source of phosphates, it is useful to mix into the soil beneath plants to help with their root development, but it can occasionally cause havoc because it is attractive to dogs and foxes. It is certainly evil-smelling stuff as you might expect, and I have always taken great care to wear gloves when handling it and not to inhale it. There are other forms of phosphates – superphosphate (inorganic) and rock phosphates (organic) – that you can use instead. But again, in theory, if you use enough organic stuff on your soil, you probably don't really need to use a separate phosphate fertiliser anyway. As is often the case, it is a question of personal choice, not a question of right or wrong.

Mycorrhizal fungi

A word or three, without too much blinding science, about mycorrhizal fungi: occurring naturally in the soil, these beneficial fungi attach themselves to the roots of plants and, in a symbiotic relationship, give plants the equivalent of a secondary, extensive, highly efficient root system, enabling them to hold on to water and extract nutrition from the soil in difficult conditions. After years of research boffins found a way to provide growers and gardeners with these fungi in dried form (sold as Rootgrow). Sprinkled in the soil at planting time or made into a dipping-slurry, mycorrhizal fungi enable bare-rooted roses (and other shrubs) to become established and grow extremely quickly. Using mycorrhizal fungi is also now believed to be helpful in preventing 'rose sickness' – a little understood soil problem all too often encountered when planting a new rose in place of an old one, that completely stops the new rose from getting going.

22

SOIL pH

There are two facts about plants that seem to stick in people's minds, even if they claim to know little else about them. One is that 'clematis needs shaded roots', and the other is that 'camellias need acid soil'. The subject of clematis I will deal with later (see pages 71–8), but it is amazing that, in a whole section on soil, I have as yet barely touched on the one thing about the subject people seem to think so important.

The acidity or alkalinity of soil (its pH value) is generally thought to be something fundamental to do with soil fertility, but it is not. It is really a question of some plants being fussy about the pH of the soil around their feet. If it is unsuitable for them, they are unable to take up nutrients from the soil and become sick and may even die. It has to be said that relatively few plants are extremely fussy, and that the vast majority of plants can cope with, or adapt to, their site.

Determining pH

Soil pH is measured on a scale of 1 to 14. Soil with a low pH (under 7) is known as acid. Soil with a high pH (over 7) is known as alkaline. Soil above chalk or limestone can be very alkaline, while the soil on land that is, or was once, heathlands and deciduous woodlands tends to be acid. If you really want to know your soil pH, then you can buy little test kits similar to those for soil fertility. Remember that you would have to take several samples from various parts of the garden to get a true picture.

It has always struck me that the general panic about soil pH is a bit of a storm in a teacup. You tend to know if you live in an area where the soil has an extreme pH, one way or another, by looking at what grows well in neighbouring gardens. Furthermore, you can often work out a plant's likely preference by thinking about where it came from originally. A plant such as sage grows naturally in thin soil on rocky hillsides (alkaline), while a camellia comes from leafy deciduous woodland (acid). Thus you would be on a hiding to nothing to attempt to grow rhododendrons (a group of plants known to be pH fusspots) if you lived in the middle of the totally unsuitable chalk downs of the south of

England, for example. Plant reference books and information websites will usually tell you if a plant has extreme preference for acid or alkaline soil, as will plant labels.

How to spot a problem

The problems, I think, arise with pH when you have soil that is not extreme, so that you can grow just about anything, but a few plants (almost always the acid-lovers) start to complain. Certain acid-loving shrubs – the camellias and rhododendrons I have already mentioned – show their distaste for too-alkaline growing conditions by developing yellowing leaves with prominent green veins, which are classic symptoms of iron-deficiency chlorosis. This can be treated with an iron tonic, such as Sequestrene, or by occasional feeding with a liquid feed specifically formulated for acid-loving plants, which acidifies the soil with iron and feeds the plant at the same time.

All evergreens (including camellias and rhododendrons) have an alarming habit of dropping loads of their older leaves at the end of the spring after flowering, just as they are putting out their new green shoots. Generally the leaves go bright yellow before they drop. This is entirely normal and it is an evergreen shrub's way of having a little 'autumn' on the quiet, so don't rush for the iron tonic. If you have any doubts about chlorosis, look at the newest leaves. If they are a good healthy green, everything in the garden is rosy, as it were.

I should also add that chlorosis is not just a symptom of iron deficiency. A languishing magnolia in my old garden, where the soil was slightly acid so it should have been happy, shrugged off all attempts to cheer it up with the addition of iron as described above. A local gardening friend had seen the problem before and suggested that the young tree was suffering from a lack of magnesium (one of the trace elements also necessary for plant growth) and told me to spray its leaves with Epsom salts. Hey presto – it subsequently thrived, only as luck would have it, to have its flower buds wrecked by late frosts every other year thereafter. Sometimes I go off gardening.

To sum up: go with the flow. Acquire a rough idea of your soil pH by looking around you at neighbouring plants. If you must grow plants that are bound to be unhappy with your conditions, grow them in containers or specially prepared raised beds in ericaceous compost (see page 35). And remember that not every yellowing leaf in the garden is down to lack of iron as a result of low soil pH.

I have compiled two short lists of shrubs that have specific pH preferences:

Shrubs for very alkaline soil

Artemisia	Brachyglottis (formerly Senecio)
Buddleja	Caryopteris
Ceratostigma	Cistus (some)
Cotoneaster	Deutzia
Euonymus	Forsythia
Hebe	Helianthemum
Lavender	Philadelphus
Phlomis	Potentilla
Rhus typhina	Rosemary
Rugosa roses	Salvia
Santolina	Thyme
Weigela	

Shrubs for very acid soil

Acer	Amelanchier
Azalea	Camellia
Cornus (some)	Enkianthus
Eucryphia	Fothergilla
Hydrangea	Kalmia

Magnolia   Mahonia
Nyssa   Pachysandra
Pieris   Rhododendron
Skimmia

COMPOST

The word compost is a pretty useless one, if the truth be told. Corrupted from the French *compote* and stirred into the English language pot, it is one of those words that is meaningless on its own, and has to be qualified at length lest it cause considerable confusion to us poor gardeners. Woe betide he or she who confuses home-made compost with soil-based or even peat-/peat substitute-based materials using the same name. You absolutely mustn't get your John Innes Nos 1, 2 and 3 composts muddled up. What is horse-manure compost composed of? What makes one compost 'organic', and another not? And what, then, is tree- and shrub-planting compost? Or ericaceous compost? Is the stuff they call multi-purpose compost truly what it says it is? First, we will look at the goodies – 'gardener's gold' – that we can make ourselves.

Home-made compost

Free food for soil is a subject close to my heart. For years I have been trying to convince owners of even tiny gardens that it really is worth saving all their trimmings, clippings and sweepings, and storing them in an orderly manner in one part of the garden. While it would be rather grand to call these garden-waste bins 'compost heaps', it is possible to rot organic matter down after a fashion and then to return the resulting brown stuff to their garden soil, in however small a quantity. This is essentially what composting is all about.

Once you have acquired the habit of composting your garden waste instead of throwing it in your council green bin without thinking, you will find it comes as second nature to scale the whole operation up if and when you get a bigger garden.

I find it all wrong to use one of those garden vacuum cleaners that seem to take up residence in the sheds of even the smallest of gardens (next to the equally noisy and eco-unfriendly power washer, as often as not), unless they are used specifically to collect and shred garden debris in order to rot it down, and so return it to the soil in composted form. I was under the impression that a lot of us garden obsessively in order to get away from the Hoover...

As I said earlier, in order to thrive plants need organic matter in the soil. Most of our gardens are deficient in it owing to over-cultivation year after year. The best way to improve the health and vitality of your garden and of your plants is to increase the amount of organic matter in the soil. Think of hedgerows and grass verges: they are fertile, vibrant and full of flowers, year after year, as a result of their own greenery dying down and rotting back into the soil to feed everything. It stands to reason that by scurrying around trying to keep our gardens as neat as new pins for twelve months of the year, and throwing out all the old vegetation with the council green bin, we are robbing our soil of its own natural food – which is, after all, free.

What equipment do I need?
Broadly speaking, there are two main types of compost container on

27

offer. Firstly, there are slatted wooden ones. Some of those sold in kit form do not work very well – simply because the slats are too widely spaced so the compost dries out and doesn't rot down very well without a bit of fussing, mixing the compost around and even watering it. They look pleasing, however, and are therefore easy to live with. Ideally the wide-slatted ones should be lined (with old potting-compost bags, maybe) and they should all be covered to keep in the naturally generated warmth and moisture (off-cuts of butyl pond liner are useful here). Secondly, there is a variety of lidded plastic bins on the market and provided at low cost by local councils. They work very well but most of them are ugly and therefore not so easy to live with.

'Hot' composting

There are two basic ways of rotting things down. One method, which can be quite quick, uses the natural heat resulting from large volumes of greenery being put all at one time into a lidded container (be it a lined wooden one or a plastic bin). If you have a shredder this method is ideal. I put all my hedge trimmings and shredded shrub prunings into a black plastic bin that looks like a Dalek without its sink-plunger. The bins heat up amazingly fast and, regularly stirred with a compost aerator, and with occasional additions of shredded paper or cardboard to sop up some of the trapped moisture, I can get a load of useful well-rotted stuff from them in about six months.

'Slow' composting

The other, more usual 'slow' method, involves the activity of moulds, bacteria and worms, and so forth, and takes up to a year to yield anything worth using. (Although you can speed things up a little by using a biological compost accelerator such as Biotal.)

It works as follows: ideally the heap needs to be at least a cubic metre (yard) in volume; if it is any smaller, the process takes even longer. Furthermore there should really be only about a 10cm (4in) layer of any one thing (such as grass clippings, snipped-up prunings or kitchen vegetable waste) put in at a time. If you are going to use kitchen waste, make sure that it is not contaminated with meat otherwise it could attract rats.

You should occasionally turn the outside edges into the middle of the heap, add the odd layer of garden soil and perhaps a compost accelerator. You should check that the heap is not too dry in the summer, especially if you have hidden it under a tree or behind a shed, and occasionally water it. In winter, you should cover the heap with a piece of old carpet underlay, or similar, to stop it getting too wet.

It may all seem like a bit of a palaver, but it works, and once the compost heap is full to the top, the fun bit starts. You turn the top (probably still un-rotted) bit over to 'bury' it a bit, add a layer of soil, climb on top of the whole thing and jump on it to compact it. To my chagrin, years ago my neighbour actually espied me doing this early one morning – yes, in my night attire.

Ideally, whatever your composting method, you should aim to have two heaps next to each other, so that one can be filled while the other finishes rotting. Remember that if a compost heap is working well, it doesn't smell foul – just a bit earthy. If it starts to stink, this means it has gone wet and sludgy in the middle – usually because there are too many grass clippings (or cold wet kitchen waste) in it. The problem may be easily fixed if you add more shredded paper or straw, if you have some.

What not to add

Is there anything that can't go in the heap? Thoroughly dry off the roots of perennial weeds such as bindweed and ground elder in the sun before you put them in your compost in case they start to re-grow and infest it. Similarly, you should try to avoid putting in weeds (that can include prolific seeders such as fennel and verbascum) that are in flower or have gone to seed. Woody trimmings should be snipped up into 5cm (2in) lengths. I suppose I should advise against putting any unwanted dug-up bulbs in there as well, or they will come back to haunt you.

One final thought: I keep an old flowerpot on the ground by my heaps. In it I chuck all the old bits of wire, old plastic plant labels and other non-biodegradable dross that gets kicked endlessly around most gardens. There is nothing more annoying than having to pick out old plant labels from otherwise beautifully made compost. If nothing else, it comes as an unwelcome reminder of just how many plants you have killed over the years and how much they cost you.

What about a wormery?

The easiest way to compost kitchen waste is to have a small three-tiered wormery – a sealed unit that contains thousands of unseen worms who will munch their way through an extraordinary amount of the stuff – outside your kitchen door. Into this you can put all manner of veg waste, shredded paper, etc. The end product is some sludgy compost (a great natural activator for a regular compost bin or heap), and loads of nitrogen-rich brown liquid that makes a great water-in plant feed if diluted with water 10 to 1.

What can I do with cooked leftovers?

There is a composting system using bokashi bran mixed, in a sealed container, with molasses and inoculated with all sorts of microthings (yeasts, fungi, certain bacteria) to break down cooked food. Even meat, fish and cheese – ingredients that you simply can't put directly into a normal compost heap or bin (because of rats) or wormery (because worms would turn up their noses at it) can be turned into something that can be added to the soil or to a regular compost bin.

Leafmould

You can, and should, make compost from falling leaves so never chuck them out, and please, please never burn them. Fallen leaves are Mother Nature's other free gift to the gardener. If you have a bit of space, pen them up in a chicken-wire cage and leave them to rot. Dead leaves rot down in a completely different way to green garden waste and are best kept separate from it. They take much longer to rot, but a year or two later you have a wonderful supply of this crumbly brown stuff known as leafmould, that looks, feels and smells divine – like a damp woodland. If you do not have the space for a 'cage', bag up your leaves (make sure they are damp), puncture the bags and hide them for a year or more where you can't see them, under evergreen shrubs or behind the shed. I use neutral-to-acid leafmould to mulch (see below) my lime-hating plants.

Mulching

Both home-made compost and leafmould are ideal for mulching – which is another of those words that needs a bit of explaining.

A mulch is a layer of material, generally but not always organic, that is spread over the surface of the soil to perform various useful functions.

Organic mulches such as home-made compost, rotted animal manure, leafmould, mushroom compost or composted bark help to keep down weeds, retain and conserve moisture and protect plant roots from frost. They also help to feed plants as the mulch breaks down into the soil. However, these 'foody' mulches, as I call them, have to be applied much more thickly than you think in order to do an efficient job. Ideally they should be 8–10cm (3–4in) thick, and applied or topped up every year in the spring, when the soil below is thoroughly moist.

Inorganic mulches such as gravel, black plastic sheeting or planting membrane, conserve moisture and/or suppress weeds. Fine gravel mulched round the necks of plants that hate British winter wet – alpines and so forth – helps to stop them rotting away.

I would love to say that I mulch all my beds and borders every year, but I don't, because it is enormously expensive and time consuming to do, and it would inhibit the self-seeding around of easy garden plants that I really like. But I do mulch all newly planted shrubs and plants with as rich and foody a mulch as I can muster, particularly those planted in the spring, in order to give them a good start in life. But if it is practicable to mulch everywhere and you have an on-going weed problem, then you should. Over a period of time, as the mulches rot down even further they become part of your topsoil, and do an immense service to all your plants.

A note to slack gardeners: it is not a good idea to put greenery – fresh lawn clippings or shreddings – directly on to flowerbeds as a mulch. While it acts as a good moisture-retentive layer, green waste can heat up as it starts to rot, scorching plant stems. And it actually takes nitrogen out of the soil it is lying on as part of its rotting-down process. Nor is it a good idea just to leave piles of leaves where they get blown in the autumn on to flowerbeds to rot in situ. All they will do is act as duvets for a rampantly hungry slug and snail population throughout the winter. You will lose your dormant delphiniums and your hostas will appear almost pre-shredded, sure as eggs.

THE OTHER SORT OF COMPOST – IN BAGS

As I indicated earlier, the word compost covers just about anything brown and sold in thick plastic bags at garden centres. First of all, we should look at potting composts, or planting mediums, the sort of stuff you buy to put in plant pots, seed trays, tubs and the like. Potting composts basically come in two forms: soil-based or peat- (now almost always peat-substitute-) based.

Soil-based composts

These are frequently sold as 'John Innes composts'. The name John Innes refers not to a manufacturer but to a formula that defines the proportions of soil, peat, sand and fertilisers. There are three types. John Innes No. 1 is a light peaty/sandy mixture fairly low in nutrients, suitable for starting off seeds and cuttings. It is, helpfully, often called 'John Innes Seed and Cuttings Compost'. No. 2 is slightly more 'soily' – suitable for potting on young plants. No. 3 is grittier and richer – for mature plants and long-term container-grown shrubs. The main problem with using a soil-based compost for large containers is the weight of the filled container, especially when wet.

Peat- or peat-substitute-based composts

These do not contain soil and are, therefore, lighter to handle. They are often labelled 'multi-purpose' because, in theory, that is what they are. Personally, I find there is a huge drawback to using them. Once they dry out, they are almost impossible to wet thoroughly again. We all have, in our time, tried to revive tragic little plants of this or that, temporarily abandoned in a corner, the compost dried to a crisp and shrunken within the pot. When you water the pot, all the water comes shooting out round the side of the compost, which remains as dry as a bone – unless you spend five minutes of your precious time doing a handstand on the thing in a bucket of water while the compost gradually plumps out again.

If you have to use peat-based compost for reasons of weight, you should consider adding to it one of the gel moisture-retaining agents sold for the purpose.

A word about peat. There is an on-going rumpus in the gardening world about the removal of peat from ancient landscapes and wildlife habitats for commercial purposes, and most responsible gardeners have stopped, or almost stopped, using it. There are substitutes – many previously 'peaty' composts now contain coir, bark or some such, and gardeners seem unable to agree as to whether they are as good as, or better than, peat. You can choose how 'green' you want to be, but certainly you should never add pure peat to your soil in bulk as a conditioner, as previous generations did: peat has no 'food value' whatsoever.

What should I use?

An enormous amount of research goes on to try to prove that this or that compost gives the 'best' results – you can hardly open a gardening magazine without seeing a series of photos of pelargoniums or something similar in plastic pots ailing to a greater or lesser degree because they haven't been grown in such and such a product. It is, as you might have guessed, absolutely not the purpose of this book to precis the latest findings of the back-room boffins. I will just stick my neck out and describe what works for me.

Seeds and cuttings

For seeds and cuttings I use peat-free multi-purpose compost with added sand to improve drainage, or John Innes Seed and Cuttings Compost (No. 1). For potting on (the next stage on for small plants) I use a mixture of about 50/50 of multi-purpose compost and soil-based John Innes No. 2. I have parched a few loved ones to within a millisecond of death on more than one occasion, but on the whole I am quite caring and fussy about small plants that I have propagated myself, and they get the best of my (generally scatty) attention.

Long-term containers

When preparing serious containers for long-term residents I generally mix three parts John Innes No. 3 (the chunky, grittier one) with one part multi-purpose compost to lighten it slightly and to increase its sponginess. If I haven't any multi-purpose compost to hand, I add one part of home-made compost (if I have enough to spare) or use spent mushroom compost, which does a similar job. I find that John Innes No. 3 on its own tends to become rather rock-like when it settles in the container. A newly planted-up big container full of fresh compost of this kind has enough nutrients in it for about a couple of months or so.

Thereafter you will have to start feeding. What I would definitely not use for container planting is ordinary garden soil or bought-in bagged topsoil – the first because it would contain weed seeds and soil pests, and the second because it is such an unknown quantity, or, should I say, quality – both in terms of pH and richness.

It goes almost without saying that you should buy any bagged compost from a source that has a quick turnover of such products, since bagged-up composts definitely deteriorate with age. They should be just very slightly damp with a nice earthy smell. If, when you open up the bags, the contents are very wet or green with algae, take them back to the place you got them, put on your best assertive smile and get your money back.

These growing mediums should not be confused with all the other things in bags, a selection of which is described below. I include this caveat only because the husband of someone I know once mulched his entire garden to the depth of 3 inches with a well-known brand of multi-purpose compost. Apparently he did think at the time that this was a rather expensive way to fertilise and mulch his garden. Indeed it was.

Compost for lime-hating plants
Erica is the Latin name for heather – a lime hater. Hence the rather odd name of the compost. Ericaceous compost is lime-free and is sold mostly for use in containers and raised beds where you intend to grow rhododendrons, camellias, heathers and others in that tribe of lime-haters. I also use it together with a little bonemeal when planting them in the open ground if I have no neutral-to-acid compost such as leafmould available.

Soil improvers
Blended horse-manure compost comprises horse manure mixed with hop waste, straw, peat or wood-shavings, with bonemeal added. It is good to plant with, but pricey. The fact that it says 'compost' on the bag means that it is well rotted and ready to use, unlike horse manure proper, which must be at least six months out of the horse and smell-free before it comes anywhere near plants.

Chicken-manure compost is organic, highly smelly, very rich in nutrients, but not as bulky as horse-manure compost. Remember it is the bulk of these composts that is needed to improve our soil as much as the goodies within them. The same goes for anything containing cow manure. I would use these as spring-time top-dressing fertilisers – feeding the plants at a time when they need it most.

Shrub- and tree-planting compost is what it says it is. If you have no home-made compost, leafmould – the 'gardener's gold' I referred to earlier – or well-rotted horse manure, this is the next best thing. Often it is recycled green waste, as produced by an increasing number of local councils, and can also be used for general mulching.

Composted bark is not very foody but is an excellent soil bulker and has a low pH, so it is good for acid-loving plants. Other bark products (coarse chippings, for example) make a good but rather untidy mulch but take for ever and a day (up to five years to be precise) to break down into the soil and provide something useful for the plants.

CHAPTER 3

Shrubs – including corrective guidelines for habitual abusers

I feel sorry for shrubs. I think they are going through a bad patch, historically speaking. For years our Victorian and Edwardian forefathers looked upon them with affection, reverence even. The 'shrubbery' was a calm and serious place for contemplative perambulation, a place to relax and unwind after a hard day's empire building. It was a sombre place where you could rest your eyes, so frequently dazzled in other parts of the garden, by garish bedding schemes and, as garden fashion shifted, blazing displays of roses.

There was another burst of enthusiasm for shrubs of a totally different kind after the Second World War, a burst that lasted well into the 1980s. Shrubs and dwarf conifers were seen as labour saving, and the idea of low-maintenance gardening took hold. The legacy is with us today. Little blue and gold conifers planted as eye-catching features now loom monstrously over many a suburban home, blocking out the light and turning the surrounding soil into a dark, lifeless desert.

Despite years of bad press, sky-high conifer hedges still blight suburban boundaries. Now ancient shrubs with sharply contrasting foliage of plum, lime-green and grey, lean mop-headed and oversized in countless once-colourful mixed borders, looking distinctly old-fashioned. Having squeezed out the peonies and smothered the phlox, they just sit there, their congested branches half-heartedly snipped at from time to time by nervous owners anxious not to do anything to upset the overwhelmingly leafy status quo.

Investing time and patience

And what are the New Gardeners up to? Forgive me if I didn't embrace the fad for stainless-steel garden structures and feature walls made out of broken council paving stones, or whatever. I am rather glad all that passed me by without my feeling obliged to join in.

The only breaking of new ground that goes on in my garden involves a spade and a wheelbarrow – I intensely dislike this endless quest for instant gratification in gardening, which seems to be leaving lovely shrubs out in the cold. Shrubs take time and patience. They don't really look any good for at least a year or two and they never fulfil their potential and eventually grumble if they are grown in pots. So they are definitely not 'here today and gone tomorrow' plants – unless you manage to kill them, that is. How many times have I walked past front gardens with a once-pretty shrub with lofty potential languishing in a 30cm (12in) tall fake terracotta pot, gasping for water and space?

The garden's backbone

I strongly believe that anyone who has any sensitivity for the way in which gardens relate to our natural landscape must appreciate that shrubs are the backbone of any garden worth the name. They form, if you like, the stylised hedgerows in the stylised meadows that grown-up gardens generally represent. I know it is not quite the same if you are gardening in an inner-city courtyard or in the Scottish highlands, or on treeless chalk downs, but I am sure you get the general drift. Peace and space: that is what we need from our gardens, and to my mind that has to involve at least a shrub or two.

Most of us, I would like to think, faced with a brand new or sparsely planted garden with no 'soul', know instinctively that a tree and a few large shrubs will make all the difference. But how do you go about it in a small space? Many of us, conversely, have gardens where the existing shrubs have taken over, and are both out of sorts and out of shape. We really need to thin them out and learn how to prune before the garden can move on.

This is, therefore, how I will tackle the subject of shrubs. How do you choose them and buy them, how do you plant them, and what do you do with them once they have become established? There is no magic formula, because our tastes and our gardens differ so wildly. But hopefully the guidelines I set out will help you to think about the whole business of shrubs in a more optimistic and constructive way.

CHOOSING SHRUBS

I simply can't do this for you since this is not that kind of a book. But there are loads of books and websites out there that can help. Here are some basic pointers you should take into account.

Sun or shade?

It is really important to know whether shrubs need sun or shade before you set your heart on them. Approaching things from the other direction, you ought to understand what is meant by sunny and shady, when applied to gardens.

Few small gardens are really sunny, simply by virtue of the fact that they have a two- or three-storey house looming over them. Boundary fences and walls can also create this sort of roof-less shade in which plants get quite a lot of light from above, but not all that much direct sun. All in all, there may well be only one area, sometimes inconveniently in the middle of the plot or in one corner that you call your 'sunny bit'. However much you may fib to yourself, this may only get a few hours of sun anyway. In winter it may even get none at all. This hardly constitutes a scorched Provençal hillside, and yet we all fantasise about growing lavender, cistuses and all that sunny stuff in inappropriate places. Crazy. Grown without pretty much full sunlight, otherwise stunning cistuses will always lean and stretch across the garden and look gaunt and ugly, however much you tie them up and try to prune them into shape.

In addition to limited direct sunshine, many gardens have areas that are dominated by nearby trees, giving dappled shade to whole tracts of garden at various times of the day. As leaf canopies thicken up as summer progresses, these areas, generally with root-riddled soil as well, can then become virtually no-go areas for other plants. Come the spring, however, when the trees are leafless and the whole garden bathed in light, we all forget about the problem and start planting the barren areas anew. There are, it has to be said, an awful lot of ways to waste your time and money in gardening! I will address the problem of planting under trees later in this book.

Natural habitat

So think carefully when choosing a shrub. It isn't just a question of light and shade; but also the natural habitat of the plant. Does it originate in the dry, airy, sharply draining hillsides of southern Europe? Does it require the temperate moisture of its native New Zealand, or is it a woodland plant, used to the overhead protection of deciduous trees, with a leafy acid soil in which to put its roots? Plant directories will tell you all this, and it is indeed important information to assimilate.

Plants work best if you can provide them with conditions similar to those they are used to in the wild, and they can cause immense problems if you try to resist going with the flow. An azalea will look as sick as a dog on a stony, sunny bank, and a curry plant will wither to nothing in the shade of an oak tree. Furthermore, it should go without saying that plants that come from the same neck of the woods, as it were, associate well together. Think how jarring on the eye a border accommodating both lavender and rhododendrons would be.

How big should shrubs be?

If you are starting with a sparsely planted garden or part of the garden, buy at least one bigger shrub or small tree to give a sense of height. This is altogether encouraging and makes you feel a lot better about spending so much money. Indeed, it may bite into the budget a bit, but it will cover more naked soil as well. I am not, on the whole, an advocate of the 'fill a juggernaut with mature trees and plant a jungle' school of gardening, partly because it is a bit of a cheat, but mostly because it is one hell of a risk. Very large shrubs sometimes don't establish well at all, chiefly because their root system is already mature within their enormous pots and may not grow out into the surrounding soil successfully once planted. However, just one or two splendiferous specimens can lift the whole game.

Inexperienced gardeners have great problems getting to know the relative heights of plants, and this is made far worse by the fact that containerised garden centre shrubs are for the most part and for convenience, generally about the same size as each other. Again, plant books and web directories will help a lot, as will reading the generally informative labels on the plants themselves. However, some plants are tortoises and some are hares, and there is no way round this problem. Beautifully scented *Daphne odora* and some of the smaller camellias grow only a few centimetres each year, while *Cistus* × *purpureus* for example, *Phlomis fruticosa*, *Lavatera* 'Barnsley' and *Buddleja davidii* are rapid space-fillers. You just have to use your loaf when spacing the plants and acquire a bit of grown-up patience. Becoming a dab hand at transplanting and eventually at pruning, is also important.

Evergreen or deciduous?

Remember that a garden will give you more to look at for longer throughout the year if you include some evergreens. Thirty per cent of the total number of shrubs in the garden is the figure often bandied about. At least 30 per cent, I would say, preferably more. The real winners are evergreen shrubs that have good flowers as well. Most are familiar players such as cistuses, choisya, the many hebes and such, and there is nothing wrong with that. There is no point in getting sniffy about them just because everyone grows them. Every garden needs its solid, reliable, multi-function work-horse shrubs. Any rare and vulnerable stuff you fancy can come later, when you know what you are doing.

The pros and cons of variegation

Variegated shrubs, with green/yellow or green/cream leaves are loved by some and loathed by many. They have been bred from naturally occurring freaks of nature, and are always less vigorous than their green relations. Inserted into gardens in moderation, they can brighten dull corners and lift the dreary days of February considerably. Beware rogue green shoots that may appear as the shrubs get bigger, and remove them at source or the shrub will eventually revert to plain green. This is particularly problematic with the *Euonymus* and *Elaeagnus* tribes, in my experience.

A word of warning: golden-leaved shrubs, both evergreen and deciduous, need particular conditions. They should be planted so they do not get the midday sun. Otherwise they bleach out (as in the case of many a sad *Choisya* 'Sundance') or scorch and go brown and hideous (alas, poor *Philadelphus coronarius* 'Aureus'). If you already have these shrubs and they are in the wrong place, move them if at all possible (see pages 50–1 for how to do this). Otherwise they will always be an eyesore.

What else should you look for?

Especially if you have a small garden, try to choose shrubs that have more than one of the following things going for them: colourful or otherwise dramatic leaves, interesting winter stems, scented flowers, evergreen leaves, good autumn tints, bright berries (see Shrubs that are 'Good Doers', page 44).

You can get caught out, however, if you don't do your homework. For example, if you are limited in space, it would be foolhardy to plant one of the huge philadelphuses (gaunt and ugly bushes whatever you do with them, but with those heavenly scented white flowers in June that evoke the smell of childhood summers). The best medium-sized philadelphus is probably *P.* 'Belle Etoile'. You could try planting the variegated version (*Philadelphus coronarius* 'Variegatus'), the golden-leaved version (*P. coronarius* 'Aureus'), the fairly compact *P. microphyllus* or even the little dwarf *P.* 'Manteau d'Hermine'. But not the big chaps, not in a small space anyway.

Another example of this sort of choice is with cornus (often known as dogwood). These wonderful foliage shrubs (the flowers are nothing much to write home about) are also loved for their red winter stems. They really look their best seen from a distance, in mass plantings in huge gardens, where they are cut to ground level at the end of the spring to create a whole new crop of shoots for the following winter, but they have a place in small gardens too.

The plain green-leaved one (with really bright winter stems) is, well, just big and plain green in the summer. The ones to grow, I think, are the coloured-leaved varieties, *Cornus alba* 'Elegantissima' (green and white) or *C. alba* 'Spaethii' (green and yellow). And don't cut them down completely in the spring, like 'big gardeners' do, unless you want to create a very strange hole in the garden structure. What works for me with cornus, in addition to a tidy-up and shape-up each spring, is to cut out one or two stems from near the base of the plant in the middle of the summer. The new shoots that are produced towards the end of the growing season are a good fresh red, the shrub doesn't get over-large, and the garden retains its 'shape' all the year round.

These are just two examples of shrubs that have more than one function, offering you a lot in one go. It is very often a question of leaf colour, but there is also the question of a plant's growth habit. This is where careful research, label reading and a touch of Latin help a great deal. A final word of caution on this subject: beware of *Ceanothus thyrsiflorus* var. *repens*. It may look to you like the answer to a maiden's prayer – a small ceanothus (most of them get huge very quickly and provide nervous pruners with an annual nightmare). The *'repens'* bit of the name means 'I am going to lie on the ground like a sulking hippo when I am not flowering.' You have been warned.

SHRUBS THAT ARE 'GOOD DOERS'

These so-called 'Good Doers' (a favourite gardening term among those 'in the know') include:

Amelanchier, which has delicate white blossom, little maroon fruits (birds permitting) and leaves that colour ravishingly in the autumn.

Photinia 'Red Robin', a fast-growing evergreen useful for informal hedges with startling scarlet young shoots.

Rugosa roses (after all, roses are shrubs, too), have scented flowers followed by scarlet hips the size of small tomatoes and bright yellow autumn leaf colour. And unlike other roses they are disease-resistant.

Sarcococcas are small, compact evergreens that are totally shade tolerant and carry highly fragrant flowers in January.

Shrubby potentillas (oh not them again!) may seem to have only one thing going for them it is true, but it is an important thing: they probably have the longest flowering season of any garden shrub.

Even common-or-garden rosemary and lavender have more to them than meets the nose, providing welcome structure to a winter garden.

BUYING SHRUBS

Not so long ago, certainly in my parents' gardening days, shrubs – deciduous ones at least – used to be bought by mail order direct from nurseries in winter, bare-rooted and dormant and had to be planted well before they acquired their leaves in spring. This instilled in that generation a certain discipline – planting was only ever done at the 'right' time. Now shrubs are generally supplied all the year round in 1- or maybe 2-litre plastic pots, in which they may have spent their entire lives since they were taken as cuttings in a nursery. Grown and supplied this way, they are generally at their best if they are about eighteen months old, after which they can become pot-bound (which means their roots become cramped) and can deteriorate if not potted on straight away to a larger container or planted out in a garden.

Although autumn is generally regarded as the best time for planting container-grown deciduous shrubs in the garden, you can plant them at any time of the year, as long as you take the necessary precautions of disturbing their roots as little as possible, watering and keeping a general eye on them for the first few months after planting. Evergreen shrubs, many of which are tender, are happier if they are planted in the spring so that they can find their feet and get established before their first real winter.

Watch out for plants sold in much larger pots (with an appropriately hiked up price). These may well just be very old 1-litre pot-dwellers that have simply been re-potted in fresh compost to cover the weeds and mossy mess in the top of the old pot. This practice is not as prevalent as it was, because we punters are all a lot smarter, but it still happens, I assure you.

Big isn't always best

It is not necessarily a good idea to home in on the biggest shrub in the batch at the garden centre, since it may have been under the most stress, having grown too big for its boots as it were. It is better to look for the chubbiest-looking plant with the strongest new growth, the best leaf colour, with no sign of pests (snails or aphids, for example) and no roots trying to escape out of the bottom of the pot. These are the real health indicators.

And one other thing: if you are like me, you will pull all the plants out on to the path in the nursery to chose the right-shaped plant for the situation you have planned for it. Plants find their own shape eventually – obviously – but you don't want to start off with an ugly duckling in your little brood. Remember to put the rejects back or the manager of the garden centre will be after you with a broom stick.

Increasingly, the giant garden centre chains sell us 'wonder plants' (my name for them). These plants are somehow spotlessly pest-free and in perfect condition. There is little to choose between a batch of twenty or so of the same thing. I find the sight of such uniformity depressing, although I know it is supposed to represent 'progress' in gardening – in the same way that straight cucumbers and perfectly uniform-sized legs of New Zealand lamb were supposed to represent 'progress' in food.

Gardeners should make sure, however, that these plants are properly 'hardened off', introduced to harsher outdoor conditions gradually, so that they will be able to cope with the weather to which they will be exposed once they leave the cosseted environment of the propagation tunnel or garden centre. In my experience, these perfect plants can go downhill before they go up, as it were.

Do your research first

Whatever you do, bone up on the shrubs you want before you go shopping. None of us can make proper shopping lists for plants and the acknowledged weakness for impulse buying is half the fun. But, before you buy, you really should know if that innocent little marvel you tuck into your trolley on the way to the checkout will turn out to be a 2m (6½ft) hooligan within two years, or whether it will languish behind the choisya (or whatever), with which you imagine it could look so good, and never be seen again.

The best garden centres and nurseries generally have someone around somewhere who is knowledgeable, happy to chat and advise. The very best also often have a lovely big dog-eared plant book under the counter that you can dip into if needed. Failing this, I think we should all make a concerted effort to break the British mould and talk to other customers in garden centres, instead of wheeling our trolleys around, whispering nervously to our partners or frowning silently to ourselves. We can learn from each other's experience. It is, after all, what you are supposed to be doing as you read this book.

Look online

Here is as good a place as any to put in a tiny word about the use of the internet. There are, at time of writing, at least a couple of useful gardening phone apps and the whole app area is mushrooming. Garden Mentor, for example, is basically a plant directory chock-full of useful cultural information that helps you choose all manner of plants for your garden (not just shrubs). The old trick of asking Google questions is sometimes helpful, although it may too often take you to US gardening forums which are of limited use here – and you should recognise that some (but by no means all) forums are full of people swapping information that is, not to put too fine a point on it, utter bunkum.

And I must give a little plug here for an indispensable source of information, online or as a book that is updated every year, called the *RHS Plant Finder*. This is a list of plants with a directory of nurseries, often tiny and specialised, where they can be bought countrywide (most do mail or internet orders) and it is invaluable if you are trying to find an obscure plant. I don't know how any plant-loving garden-maker could do without the *Plant Finder*. In the pursuit of plants, it will take you wonderful places you have never been – in every sense.

PLANTING SHRUBS AND TREES

It may sound a bit grand, but it really does help to use a wheelbarrow, especially if you have more than one shrub to plant. If you haven't got a barrow, then a thick plastic sheet on the ground where you are to work is the next best thing. Into the barrow or on to the sheet put about the equivalent (per shrub to be planted) of a bucketful of organic stuff – mushroom compost, home-made compost, rotted manure or a shrub-planting compost.

First dig your hole

Dig a planting hole for the shrub, at least twice the size of the pot in every direction, and add the soil that comes out of the hole to your pile of compost in the barrow or on the sheet. If you are going to use the soil, sprinkle a large handful of bonemeal on to it and on to the compost and mix the lot together. If you are not using the soil, use more organic stuff as explained previously in the chapter on soil (see pages 27–31).

Put about a third of the resulting planting mixture back in the hole and fork it about to incorporate it into the soil at the bottom. De-pot your shrub, having first made sure it was sufficiently damp by soaking it in a bucket of water until no air bubbles come out of the pot, and it feels therefore quite heavy. You could put soluble fertiliser in the water if you are feeling in a lavish, nurturing frame of mind.

If there are any roots coming through the holes in the bottom of the pot that are dry, brown and dead-looking you can cut them off. If they are damp, fresh and pale, try not to damage them. If the shrub was badly pot-bound – that is, if the roots look congested and 'tortured' into the pot's shape – you could gently loosen the odd one with a finger. Roots are extremely delicate things, however, and much frantic picking can do more harm than good. It is a difficult situation on which to give advice; ideally you should try to acquire plants that are not in this condition.

Then add your plant

Snuggle the root ball (that's the term for the minimally disturbed roots, plus whatever compost they are growing through in the pot) down into the soft soil/compost in the planting hole. Make sure that the junction between root and stem will end up at the same level as it was when potted (in other words, that the hole is not too deep or too shallow). If there is a problem with this, start all over again.

If not, begin to put the contents of the barrow back into the hole around the plant, firming very gently as you go. When the root ball is about half buried, water the whole area and let it drain away. Finish back-filling round the plant, firm the area with your boot (or muddy slipper) and apply an additional mulch of organic stuff. You should not need to water again for a week or so. Should there be anything left in the barrow or on the plastic sheet, it can be rolled over into the next job, and any surplus soil or planting mixture can be sprinkled under hedges or used to top up soil in borders.

Additional planting tips

Don't use bonemeal if you are the owner of a daft dog, who will try to dig up your plants thinking he has buried last night's dinner under them. Foxes will do the same. If you feel your soil could do with it, use superphosphate or rock phosphate or a balanced general fertiliser, such as Growmore, which is not quite the same thing but will do.

If you are planting in turf (a tree perhaps), take off a circle of turf first, and bury some of it upside down under the shrub or tree. You will have to dig a deeper hole to accommodate the extra bulk, but it is worth it. The old turf will rot down in situ and will act as splendid fertiliser for a few years. The plant should grow like the clappers.

If you are going to need a supporting stake (not hideous bamboo), put it in as you plant the shrub or tree. If you leave it till later you may well damage roots. Use proper tree ties or several thicknesses of Flexi-Tie tied loosely as a temporary measure (it will stretch as the tree grows, but should be checked annually).

If you are planting at the 'wrong' time – in the summer, for example – and the soil is dry at the bottom of the hole you have dug, fill it with water and let it drain. Do this a couple of times before you put in the compost/soil mixture. If the water takes a whole day to drain away, break up the bottom of the hole again, put in some grit or gravel, and add more grit to the planting mixture – you probably have clay under your soil.

If you are planting at the 'right' time, in the autumn or spring, and the hole is very dry at the bottom ... think twice about the site you have chosen.

TRANSPLANTING SHRUBS

While no serious gardener can possibly advocate playing chess with their shrubs on a regular basis, there is no doubt that learning how to transplant major players in the garden is a vital skill, the acquisition of which gives great confidence. We all tend to over-plant, to a lesser or greater extent, and shrubs invariably get overcrowded. We also change our minds, want to try out new combinations and ideas, and it would be only half the fun – and incredibly expensive – if we had to chuck out mature shrubs all the time.

Moving something after only a year is easy, since the plant's roots will barely have moved out of the original planting hole and the soft compost you provided for it. You just have to go through the motions all over again, watering the shrub well before you start and trying to disturb the roots as little as possible. Generally the shrub doesn't even notice and its growth is barely checked. Moving young shrubs around too often is not to be recommended, since they never really get going – and the garden will look restless because of it.

Moving established plants

Older shrubs need greater care. The best time to transplant mature deciduous shrubs is in the winter when they are leafless. However, I have in my time succeeded in transplanting a 2m × 2m (6½ft × 6½ft) deutzia in midsummer, which proves that nothing is impossible.

I had my greatest success with evergreens in the very late summer or early autumn, so that they have time to recover before the winter cold, and will start to grow properly again as soon as spring comes. They are trickier than deciduous shrubs since they will usually wilt for a week or two, which will inevitably freak you out. It makes sense not to move them when it is likely to be windy, or frosty, or brilliantly hot and sunny.

If you are transplanting a shrub that is really large, start by cutting it down by up to a half. Whatever time of year it is, it will recover from the inevitable shock of losing some of its roots if it does not have to support all its old top growth. It also makes the physical business of moving it easier – especially if it has thorns. You may find that, depending on the flowering time of the shrub and the time of year you 'operate', the shrub will flower poorly the next year.

So how do you actually go about it?

Drizzle a hose into the ground, overnight or at least for several hours, around the base of the shrub, a couple of days before you intend to transplant. (As a result, the root area should be damp but not mushy.) Start to dig vertically down around the shrub, remembering that roots will be spread out from the main stem about as far as its branches extend. You probably cannot realistically hope to avoid cutting the outermost roots, but you should still be aware of what proportion you will be damaging.

Once you have dug around the shrub as deeply as you can go, try gently rocking it to get a feel for where the deeper roots are going. You will probably then have an idea of how large the new planting hole should be, which you should then go and prepare – following the guidelines given for planting new shrubs. What you must avoid at all costs is digging up the shrub and leaving it lying around with its roots exposed while you dig out its new home.

Lift the shrub out of its old site – it may well mean cutting through one or more big roots – and on to a plastic sheet. Make sure the damaged root ends are cleanly cut off with no rips or snaggy bits that could rot and cause future problems. Then drag the plant to the new site. Check the new hole is the right size. It must be deep enough. Make sure that when you put the shrub in the new site it is 'facing' the right way and looks harmonious with its neighbours. This sounds silly, but if you have ever got this bit wrong, you will know what I mean.

Remember when back-filling the soil and compost that you must make sure there are no air pockets under the roots. Use your hands at first and finally tread the shrub in well and mulch thickly.

Keep a close eye on the patient, and it should, if deciduous, burst into life happily in the spring – although you may have lost a year's flowers because of having cut it back. Water it very well every two or three weeks in the growing season of the first year. Evergreens will inevitably wilt, even if it is not sunny. Depending on just how brutal you were and how big the shrub was, it will either take weeks or months for the shrub to return to its former glory. Or it may even die on you, but at least you had a go.

PRUNING SHRUBS

When it comes to pruning shrubs – as I am afraid it always must eventually – gardeners divide themselves into two camps.

There are those who, at the first whiff of spring, flex their muscles, thrust back their shoulders, grasp those Christmas-present secateurs and launch themselves into the garden. Three hours later they return, having 'tidied things up' for the year. The garden, maimed but generally not fatally wounded, takes months to recover. The ceanothus, *Clematis montana* and shrub roses don't flower, and the choisya is reduced to something resembling a set of antlers sticking out of the ground, but at least the pathways are clear and nothing hangs over the lawn to interrupt the progress of the mower. These people, caged lions in urban gardens, dream of moving to the country where they can plant lots of trees and train their children (generally sons, it has to be said) to be the next generation of axe-men gardeners, giving them plastic swords with which to chop off the heads of the rhododendrons when playing with their little friends.

Then there are those who love the romance of the overgrown jungle or the 'cottage-garden look' and blench at the sight of a pruning saw or go glassy-eyed when consulting a pruning manual. These are the gardeners who will happily plant a Russian vine to grow up a wisteria or a 'Kiftsgate' rose to go over a shed. They plant potentially thuggy *Lavatera* 'Barnsley' in groups of three and can't bear to cut them down in spring because they were 'so good last year'. When the whole garden threatens to strangle them in their beds, they cut their way into the tangle with a pair of kitchen scissors, put a bench in the resulting hole and call it an arbour. When it all gets too worrying, they put their houses on the market while everything is in flower so no one can see the mess and then get the hell out – a bit like selling the car when the ashtray is full.

It's not just a man thing...

Do not presume, however, that there is a rigid gender divide. I am the product of a mother who, when partially sighted and with a dickey left arm, still pruned for England at the age of 90. My father, on the other hand, adored growing trees and shrubs until he died, happily planting them, often with little prior discussion, slap in the middle of my mother's herbaceous borders when she wasn't looking and rarely wanting to prune them. They became the subject of acid discussions over numerous Sunday lunches as they grew more and more unsightly and out of control. Nor did the trees and shrubs look any better. My father, I am convinced, had no idea how to prune, despite his great botanical knowledge.

What follows is a serious attempt to make pruning easier for the romantic ditherers and put a curb on the most uncontrollable axe men. There are no pictures to help you. I am using no diagrams of perfect shrubs (that look nothing like your own sad wrecks) with little black marks across the branches to show you where to cut. Trust and concentrate. Then go and look at your shrubs and see if it all begins to make sense.

Everything will need pruning at some point

All mature garden shrubs – those over two or three years old – need some kind of pruning to keep them looking good. Pruning is largely a matter of common sense – the application of a few bendable rules to suit your particular requirements. If you employ outside help to do your pruning, as often as not it will be a disaster since many 'gardeners' resort to a scorched earth policy because they do not understand these rules. Even if they do, they often do not have the intimate knowledge that is needed of either your plants or the site to adapt the rules to the best advantage. There are three main methods of pruning: cutting back hard, thinning out and spur pruning.

Cutting back hard

This is what you do to LATE-flowering deciduous shrubs, those that start to flower after midsummer on the end of shoots produced during the current season. Common examples are: buddleja and lavatera. It is also often referred to as 'hard pruning'.

In very early spring (late February perhaps in the south of Britain, later in the north), cut all branches back to a woody framework, which should remain virtually unchanged over the years once the shrub is mature. The size and height of the framework depends on a) how much the shrub grows each year before it flowers and b) at what height you want to see the plant flower. For example, *Buddleja davidii* grows approximately 1.2–1.5m (4–5ft) in a year and flowers from the tips of its branches. If you wanted to keep it as small as possible, you would prune annually, to a framework of about 30cm (1ft) in height. If, however, you wanted the bush to hide a 2.5m (8ft) high garden shed, you would cut only the front branches to 30cm (1ft), staggering the framework so that the back branches would be cut down to about 1.5m (5ft). (Buddleja look wonderful treated this way, with those pointed scented flowers stretching out on the end of long supple branches. You get that heavy honey scent at nose height and upwards – lovely.) Shapes and sizes of shrubs can be quite precisely stage-managed in this way.

Cutting back is also an effective way of dealing with very overgrown shrubs that need drastic treatment, whatever their flowering period. However, if you cut back EARLY-flowering shrubs in February (as opposed to the LATE-flowering group above), there will be few, if any, flowers that year.

Less vigorous LATE-flowering shrubs, such as potentilla, lavender and hypericum, do not need drastic cutting back every year. A 'haircut' with the shears each spring is sufficient, and at the same time, you can cut out at the base any dead wood from the middle of the shrub to tidy it up.

All cutting back should be followed by heavy feeding and mulching.

Thinning out

This you do to EARLY-flowering shrubs, which flower on side shoots coming off the previous season's growth. Examples are: winter jasmine, forsythia, ceanothus, rosemary and philadelphus. Since these shrubs flower only on year-old wood, the aim is to control growth while encouraging production of more new shoots to carry flowers where they are wanted the following year. It is a subtle operation, but not difficult if you do it immediately after flowering has finished – which could be February in the case of winter jasmine, or July in the case of philadelphus.

Thinning out should be done in two stages:

1 Cut out at ground level some of the very oldest wood (the thickest and most gnarled), plus any diseased and damaged stems. 'One in three branches' is often quoted, but it depends on the type, age and condition of the shrub you are working on. When you are thinning out a neglected bush for the first time, you will probably need to use a small pruning saw. It will be hard work. What you are aiming to do is open out the base of the bush so that new, vigorous stuff has room to develop and grow up through the older stuff.

2 Shorten stems that have borne flowers back to a point at which there are some strong buds showing, even if those stems have started to put out new growth at the tip. The shoots you are removing would be naked and ugly for most of their length the following year if you left them to grow on, while the buds and shoots to which you cut back will carry next year's flowers. What you are aiming to do is keep the shrub roughly the same size overall, while ensuring the maximum number of branches carry good flowers.

If you are working on a very large shrub, keep standing back and looking at the overall appearance of the bush. The basic branch pattern should not alter much and the shrub should generally look much better and slightly smaller immediately after pruning, with the bright young shoots that will grow to carry next year's flowers in greater evidence.

If you are timid with this thinning out, the shrub will be too blowsy by the end of the summer. This is when the problems really start, with the temptation to give the shrub a short back and sides as you tidy things up in the autumn, resulting in the removal of many of the new shoots already carrying flower buds for the next spring.

Mastering the art of pruning EARLY-flowering shrubs is one of the most important jobs in a small garden, where space is generally limited and every shrub has to earn its keep to the full.

Spur pruning
This is what you do to wall-trained shrubs or climbers where space is limited. The aim is to check growth moderately while persuading the plant to produce as many flowering shoots as possible. It is quite difficult to do and even harder to explain, but in my experience few gardens contain more than one or two plants in this category – wisteria and chaenomeles (Japanese quince) are the most common examples.

In early summer, cut back all new (long and whippy, in the case of wisteria) shoots to within about six leaves of their starting point, saving only those shoots needed to create part of the permanent structure. Another crop of new shoots will then be produced during the rest of the growing season from the axils of the remaining leaves (the point where the leaf joins the stem), and these should be similarly cut back in the autumn or early winter. At the same time, the shoots that were originally cut back in the summer should be shortened even further, leaving about three buds from above their bases. Any other whippy growth that is still in evidence after you have done all this should be shortened to about 5–8cm (2–3in).

I do recommend getting help with wisteria pruning if yours is a large specimen. It is all very well being brave and self-sufficient, but it is really dangerous counting all those leaf buds up a ladder in a force nine. My parents used to have a vast wisteria with a mind of its own all over the front of their house. My father used to cut the phone wires just about every time he did the pruning. He hated doing the job, and I think he was trying to tell my mother that professional help was needed, bless him.

A rather unorthodox combination of spur pruning and thinning out can be used for some early-flowering, over-vigorous shrubs – such as forsythia, which, for some reason, always seems to be planted where there is not enough space for it – at intervals throughout the growing season. If the growing shoots are trimmed back by about a third every five or six weeks, they will still produce enough compact new growth to give a good display of flowers the following spring. It is worth experimenting once you understand the basics.

Some exceptions to the rules

Evergreens
Evergreen shrubs grown chiefly for the beauty of their foliage should have their branches shortened and thinned out and some of the oldest growth removed in March. Frost-damaged shoots should also be cut out at this time. Very vigorous shrubs or hedges can be cut again in July. Evergreens that are also grown for their significant flowers generally flower in the spring (*Viburnum tinus* and *Choisya ternata* are two examples). They should be cut back after flowering, either quite hard every other year or gently every year. If they are not pruned, you often get a surprisingly good second flush of flowers in the autumn, so the alternate year approach is more rewarding.

Late-flowering evergreens
Shrubs such as hebes and brachyglottis (formerly senecio) should have only damaged shoots and tired flower heads removed, until they get too big. Once this happens you have to cut them right back in early summer and you will get nothing – except lush leaf growth – from them until the following year. If you don't want brachyglottis to flower, treat it as an evergreen pure and simple, cutting it back each spring.

Early-flowering shrubs grown for berries
Berried shrubs such as pyracantha, for example, need sensitive handling. Prune out half of the shoots that have flowered immediately after flowering to encourage new growth for next year. Leave the other half to form berries for the blackbirds!

Hydrangeas
There is no single rule since there are so many different types. The common mop-heads and lace-caps flower best from younger wood, and

at the very least you should take out wood that is more than two years old from the base every spring. At the same time, prune down shoots that have flowered once to a pair of fat buds (somewhere in the top few inches of the shoot), but do not touch the young shoots that have not yet flowered. *Hydrangea serrata* and *H.* 'Annabelle' can be cut down to a framework each spring once they are two or three years old, since they flower well on new wood.

Lavender

Technically speaking, this is a late-flowering shrub, but it is one that gets very woody and ugly after only a few years. I trim lavender twice, as follows. Immediately after flowering, remove the flowers together with the stalks and about 5cm (2in) of each shoot; during the remainder of the summer the bush will re-grow and become a good rounded shape. The following spring prune the bush again, this time taking off about 10cm (4in) – it depends on the variety, if it is a big lavender, take off more. Do not cut right down into the old wood – that is, below the little grey whiskery shoots that you can see just emerging from the woody stems. If you do, the lavender will not flower well that year. If you have a very old lavender that is gnarled and ugly, replace it (you could try taking cuttings from it), unless of course you like the rather exotic shape of it. Formal lavender hedges should be neatly pruned to look good. I just love to walk slowly along an old path edged with dark purple lavender, heavy and humming with bees in the heat of the midday sun. It is, to my mind, one of the best garden experiences.

A final observation

Shrubs are not the only plants to which the 'early-flowering' and 'late-flowering' labels apply. The fog of confusion surrounding the subject

58

of rose pruning can be somewhat dispersed if you realise that while Hybrid Tea, climbing and Floribunda roses flower on the current season's growth, and must therefore be pruned in the spring, ramblers and shrub roses flower on the previous season's growth and should be dealt with after flowering. Similarly, there are early- and late-flowering clematis. I will deal with these in subsequent chapters of the book, but I thought I would just throw this in as food for thought.

CHAPTER 4

Walls and fences and things

Walls and fences to most gardeners mean 'climbers', but growing climbers is not always the best solution to covering walls and fences and hiding eyesores. I shall attempt to explain why.

For a start, climbers climb. Up and up. Many are woodland and hedgerow plants that, by various different means that I will describe later, climb up host trees until they reach the sun – and pollinating insects – and then they flower. The host plants provide them with nutrients in the form of decayed fallen leaves, protect their young growth from strong, drying winds and also shade their far-reaching roots, which need cool, moist root-runs and plenty of space.

Now consider the average house wall or boundary. It will very possibly be wind-swept, blisteringly hot and sunny or dank and shady, invariably with dismal soil or indeed none at all at its base. Even if it is gorgeous old brick, you will very probably be anxious to grow something all over it. Fast. There may be trouble ahead...

WALL SHRUBS

I will start this section by ignoring the actual climbers for a bit and looking at the alternatives: the shrubs, often referred to as 'wall shrubs', that do well with their backs flat against a vertical surface, perhaps tied lightly to it. Over these you have much more control than a tangle of interlocking climbers. At least you have once you understand more about pruning.

Sunny walls

House walls, especially sunny south- or west-facing ones are naturally warm and provide the most interesting planting opportunities.

Favourites include ceanothus – all sorts, mostly blue, mostly spring-flowering, mostly evergreen; *Argyrocytisus battandieri*, not evergreen and flowering a smitch later, with silvery leaves and stubby racemes (dangly bits) of pineapple-scented yellow flowers; *Rhamnus alaternus* 'Argenteovariegata', a good workhorse-type variegated-leaved evergreen that is eminently trimmable and adaptable. Likewise several pittosporums (alas slightly tender in the north) with all sorts of leaf colours from gold through variegated to dull plum. Some shrubs that you don't associate with height achieve remarkable climbing feats if tied up lightly. Brachyglottis (formerly senecio) can surprise you this way, as can *Phygelius capensis*, with its upside-down-looking orange bottle-shaped flowers in late summer: most exotic.

Shady walls

Shade is, as always, more difficult, and sun-lovers planted against shady walls will never flower as brilliantly as they would with a bit of sun, and will lean and stretch towards any light source. But with nourishment, adequate water and a bit of support, you can coax something out of spring-flowering chaenomeles (Japanese quince), or use the strong shapes of mahonia or *Fatsia japonica* (the castor oil plant) against a contrasting background. I have even seen dear old brachyglottis (see above), choisya and rhamnus trying really hard against shady walls as well.

Tying them in

In all cases, remember, if you are going to tie woody stems back on to a wall – or on to any kind of support – you must use proper shrub or tree ties, double or treble thicknesses of lightly tied garden twine or Flexi-Tie. Bits of plastic-coated electrical flex will do (as long as it is not white!) and I have even known people resort to using old tights. Never, ever, use garden wire, even as a 'temporary measure'. The chances are you will, like me in the days before Flexi-Tie, forget to go back to re-do the job until the branches in question have been severely cut into by the wire, and untold damage has been caused. Humiliating stuff.

As with so many spur-of-the moment gardening jobs, the chore of having to go and get the right tools or materials for a job is more than outweighed by the sense of virtue and well-being that comes upon you when you know that the job has been *properly* done. This is the sort of frightful stuff our grandmothers taught us, and it has taken me a surprisingly long time to find that it is true.

Vanishing boundaries

I really like wall shrubs. They add depth to the boundaries of a garden, and if you are lucky enough to have good shrubs coming over the fence or wall from a neighbour's garden, you can even make the boundary 'vanish' by planting the same things on your side. It may be just a personal quirk, but I find the sight of a larchlap fence covered by a solitary clematis rather soulless, even when – perhaps especially when – smothered in bloshy blooms the size of dinner plates. What I really, really like to see is a series of well-ordered wall-trained shrubs with climbers growing within and between, and even all over them, but not smothering them. It is not so very difficult to achieve if you choose your plants carefully and don't succumb to the temptation to grow too much, too close together in order to achieve an 'instant' result. Furthermore, you have to understand the different needs and habit of the plants involved.

But there is something about climbing plants that captures the imagination of all gardeners, and leads them astray.

CLIMBERS

These are very much the icing on the gardening cake. Allowed to ramble seemingly unaided up walls and fences, through and over other plants and features, carefully chosen so as to harmonise or contrast perfectly with their hosts, they create a magical effect – especially in small gardens where both drama and detail are so important.

So much for the fantasy. In reality, what we generally end up with is an ill-thought-out mishmash of climbers that need different pruning care, planted in the wrong place with little or no support apart from each other, cantilevered out from the over-burdened garden fence and causing serious damage in the neighbourly relations department. It can quickly become an uncontrollable nightmare. So here are some things you should know about them.

Do your homework

Firstly, *choose carefully* when planting new climbers. Rampant climbers such as *Clematis montana, C. armandii*, the dreadful evergreen honeysuckle and wisteria really do need to be given a lot of space and very sturdy support *before* they get going. As previously mentioned, they are really designed by Mother Nature to go up trees and stay up there, or even wander from tree to tree without let or hindrance for years. If you have the space to let them do this, lucky you. In smaller gardens, however, they can overwhelm and kill other shrubs (generally, of course, those belonging to your neighbour).

If you grow smaller climbers up into existing mature shrubs, remember that the pruning rules apply to all shrubby plants, including climbers. For example, do not grow a Group B clematis that needs minimal winter or spring pruning (more, and it won't flower) into a December-pruned climbing rose.

Secondly, *climbers need a good, deep root run.* That is why most of them do really badly in pots. This is an undeniable fact and one that even experienced gardeners fail to come to grips with until they have squandered a small fortune. It is also a heart-breaking fact, since so many of our gardens have areas with blank walls and fences and no soil to plant in at their bases.

Creating a planting area where none exists

The only sensible advice in these circumstances is to try to move heaven and earth and paving stones or whatever, to create a good planting area – coming out from the wall or fence by at least 60cm (2ft) with really good soil to a depth of at least 60cm (2ft). It will probably be necessary to replace completely the foul stuff that you find under the paving stones or concrete that you have removed. Alternatively you could build substantial raised beds with proper drainage, taking care if a damp-proof course is involved.

Here is a useful tip for unashamedly girlie gardeners. Always try to remove paving stones or lay bricks when there is a builder nearby, even if you know that they are fully occupied installing a tricky RSJ or gloss-painting the front door. You will undoubtedly have the club hammer or bricklayers' trowel, or whatever it is, gently taken from you and you will be shown just how it should be done. I have not actually tried bricklaying in my pyjamas, since I have always had excellent results in this department even when wearing filthy jeans and a torn wax waistcoat, looking relatively capable to boot. There are still, bless them, plenty of traditional blokes out there only too pleased to assist a damsel in distress.

Climbers in containers – if you absolutely must...

If there truly is absolutely no alternative, then grow non-rampant climbers in huge containers – half-barrels even – and remember that:

a) a climber will only go up as long as it can go down, and

b) it must never, ever be allowed to dry out.

Use a container that is as non-porous as possible and does not conduct heat well (wood is good; if it is unglazed, terracotta should be lined with plastic). Plant in John Innes No. 3 compost with a little extra organic stuff or multi-purpose compost and with time-release fertiliser granules. Cover the top of the soil with pebbles or cobbles to retain moisture. Do not be tempted to plant anything else in the tub or pot with the precious climber or it will have to compete for water and food. If you absolutely must, then stand other pots of pretties on top of the pebble layer in the barrel. This will jolly it up a bit visually, disguise the enormity of the container below and provide the major incumbent with a source of second-hand water and nutrients by draining through into the container below when you water them. Every year or so, remove the pebbles, scrape away the top few inches of soil and replace them, adding more food as well. With this gold-star treatment and much effort, you will probably succeed.

Climbers in the ground (ah, much better...)

Try to avoid shoe-horning climbers into dry bits of scrubby soil where they have to compete for food, water and root space with their intended hosts. This is especially important if the hosts are already well established and will be robbing their new young companions of all the necessities of life from day one.

If you are planting a climber – a rose or clematis, say – to go up a tree, try to plant it as far away from the trunk as possible. I find that a branch pruned from the host tree, placed on the ground and leant against the tree's lower branches, to which you loosely tie the climber, provides the most natural way to 'lead' it upwards. Remember, you will have to look at whatever you use for support for a long time. In my view nothing is worse than an alien-looking bamboo cane in this situation.

Once up in the lower forked branches of the tree, the climber will most likely find its own way up as nature intended, but you should check things from time to time and, if it is struggling, lend a helping hand by wrapping a piece of chicken wire around a branch or tying stems in loosely.

When planting near trees and shrubs, always, always, improve the soil in the planting area massively, digging down as deeply as you can, and mulch and feed for the first year while the newcomers are finding (or perhaps I should say burying) their feet.

One last thing on the subject of planting climbers. You have been dreaming idly for weeks – throughout an entire summer, maybe – of seeing cascades of flowers of some heavenly scrambler tumbling elegantly from top to bottom of some otherwise unremarkable tree at the end of the garden. You know how it is; we all do it. Come planting time in the autumn (you don't know how you managed to show such self-discipline and wait this long), you drive 30 miles to the only nursery in your part of the country that stocks your wonderful whatever-it-is. You rush home, knowing already where you are going to plant it. Start digging. Shock horror. You manage with difficulty to dig 60cm (2ft) down and still the soil is full of tree roots, dry as dust, frightful. You do what you have been told. Fill the hole with water – go off and do the crossword, drink a gallon of coffee in sympathy, whatever. More shock horror – an hour later the water hasn't drained. Oh woe, oh woe. Must be solid rock or clay underneath. Take my advice, plant your treasure somewhere else. You have just hit on the 'planting site from hell' and the plan will never work. I write as one who knows.

The right support...

Wherever, whatever and whenever you plant your climbers, they will only behave the way they should if you provide them with the *right kind of support*. If you take a good look at various types of climber, you will see that they actually have totally differing methods of scrambling upwards and benefit from differing methods of support.

I will mention roses only briefly as they are dealt with elsewhere. I should mention, however, that in the wild they use their thorns as a means of scrambling up trees and things and ramblers are quite happy to climb garden trees this way, too. But in the confines of the ordinary garden, climbers and ramblers need to be tied to supports. They should never be poked behind retaining wires or woven into trellis. The wires will soon damage the shoots and the trellis will be wrenched apart as the rose expands.

...for twiners

We are all familiar with twiners such as honeysuckle, jasmine and the dreaded wisteria (have you really got room for this seductive giant?). In fact it is amazing how many people think that all climbers do it this way. Such plants initially need vertical support. They should be untwined very carefully from the cane they have been grown up in the nursery. The stems should then be fanned out (or whatever is appropriate to the site) and encouraged to go up parallel vertical wires. You get quicker results this way. Remember you only get one shot at it, because before you can say 'Jack Robinson' your climbers will have shinned up whatever you provide for them – often things like phone wires and drainpipes that are, shall we say, less than ideal. Unless you want the whole shooting match to land on your head after a storm in a few years' time, use proper heavy galvanised wire and vine eyes to fix it to the wall.

It is not just about being sensible just for the sake of it. The plants perform – and look – a lot better. I once made the mistake of leaving a honeysuckle twined around itself and a bamboo cane, only fanning out the top growth. After a few years the bottom 60cm (2ft) looked like a massive twisted piece of rope with a tortured cane splintered and broken in its middle. It was truly ugly and can't have done its best that way.

...for petiole climbers

Petiole climbers such as clematis and *Solanum laxum* 'Album' use their leaf stalks to help them scramble about, forming what I call 'elbows' where the leaf stalk (petiole) joins the leaf and making a kind of knot around their support. (Incidentally, the blue solanum – *Solanum crispum* 'Glasnevin' – doesn't do the same thing at all. It barely supports itself, in fact, and should really be called a 'scrambler' rather than a climber. It needs to be firmly tied up and rigorously pruned.) Petiole climbers need a fairly fine mesh to grow up unless they are climbing up other plants. Oddly enough, the gauge of wood in ordinary garden trellis is too large for them, and they can end up flapping about in anything more than a gentle breeze, which will naturally slow their progress. Fairly coarse chicken wire (which you can get in either dark green or just plain galvanised metal), stapled or nailed on to fences, walls, sheds and so forth, and on the back of trellis or even wrapped around rustic poles, is surprisingly invisible. It enables the plant to create a firm base from which to ramp ever onwards and upwards.

...for clingers

Climbers such as ivy, climbing hydrangea and the lovely, exotic-looking *Campsis radicans* are clingers once they get going but need rough brickwork into which to stick their small aerial roots. They 'take' very slowly on dry, warm, wooden fences and detest most wood preservatives. If you buy a big ivy on a bamboo cane from a garden centre, do not expect the growth it already has to somehow start to stick to your walls. Once you have planted it you should take the ivy right off the cane and bury the stems in the (improved) soil along the base of the wall you are trying to cover, so that only the leaves remain visible above ground. It will make numerous new shoots along the length of each stem and these will then march up the wall at an amazing pace, giving a wide area of coverage in a remarkably short time. It will certainly be a whole lot quicker than trying to anchor the stems to the wall or worst of all, just leaning the plant, stick, plastic ties, staples and all against the wall and hoping it will find its own way in due course. Anyone blushing?

...for tendril climbers

Tendril climbers, such as grapevines and other ornamental vines, will grab at any support, turning their tendrils into little springs. Take a close look sometime: it is one of nature's marvels. They thrive best with a combination of vertical and horizontal wires about 45cm (18in) apart, forming a grid. If you want them to look smart and formal, you train them carefully on to these wires so that they make a permanent woody framework to which you prune back every winter. If you don't, they will just lurch around, grabbing anything they can latch on to. Chaos but rather nice unless space is limited. Vines live a long time, so their support wires should be strong and able to last for up to 400 years or so. You have been told.

Another annoying fact about grapevines and their ornamental relations is that, unlike most other climbers, they cannot just be lopped at if they become really untidy when they come into leaf. The flow of sap in the old wood in particular is so strong that if you cut or injure it in spring it will 'weep' uncontrollably for weeks. Instinctively, you think that the whole vine will weep to death, though apparently this is not the case. It is just not very nice to sit under a vine-covered arbour and be dripped on. All in all, I regard grapevines in small gardens as a bit of a fantasy plant for the dedicated and knowledgeable.

...for climbers with suction pads
There are climbers – Virginia creepers and various relations – that stick their little hand-like suction pads into crevices and rough stonework. They can just about climb up fences unaided, but on these and on smooth rendering they prefer help with waterproof sticky tape or a bit of Blu-Tack until they start growing strongly. If the wind blows them off their support thereafter, they generally manage to climb straight up again, although you may have to cut bits off first.

A final thought on supporting climbers. Fortunately, few of us have totally new gardens with naked walls and fences to clothe from a standing start. But often, because of plant deaths or disasters or building works or a combination of all three, boundaries and surfaces in our gardens become free for planting. In the light of experience, I think I would now immediately cover the surface with coarse chicken wire, with maybe some horizontal wires as well, even before I decided what to plant. This would give me the greatest flexibility in my choice of plants, as well as that aforementioned warm feeling of having for once done a really grown-up job.

CLEMATIS – SIMPLIFIED AT LAST

I think I should devote a special little section to clematis, because they give so many otherwise confident gardeners the habjabs. The general gist of complaints is that either they always die on you, generally almost immediately or, if they don't die, they get out of hand and you don't know what to do with them. The first problem – that of almost instant death – is about how they are planted and treated in their first year, when they need a lot of TLC. If they get past their first tricky summer, they generally improve each year thereafter.

Timing

Clematis prefer to be planted in early autumn or late spring – in other words when the soil is still warm from the summer or starting to warm up in the spring. Nurseries and garden centres get in good supplies then, so the choice should be wide. If you buy them at other times, you will most probably be shuffling through the plants all the sensible gardeners have already rejected. You should always try to find a specimen that has as much new growth near the bottom as possible.

Planting method

Clematis really *do* need to be planted in absolutely wonderful soil that has been dug deeply and enriched in advance. Young plants tend to be supplied in tall slim pots (because clematis have deep roots) and the hole you dig should be at least twice the depth of that pot, and about three times its width. In the hole should go half a bucket of 'good stuff', such as mushroom compost with a little bonemeal, or home-made compost or whatever you buy for shrub planting from the garden centre. Fork it all around to incorporate it into the surrounding soil and sprinkle some more to be mixed with the soil that will be packed back around the plant. Then fill the hole with water and let it all soak away. This takes longer than you think. (This is all fairly standard information for planting anything.)

The next bit is important. Place the un-potted clematis in the prepared hole, and make sure that the hole is deep enough so that the first 5–6cm (2–2½in) of the stem of the plant will be *under the soil* once the soil/planting compost is put back round the plant and it has all been firmed down.

The reason for this is that clematis shoots and stems are thin, brittle and vulnerable. Should there be a problem with clematis wilt (see page 73) or, as is more likely, snail or slug damage at soil level, dormant buds on the stem below soil level can shoot out from the healthy root system and all will not be lost.

Watering in the early stages

Having been deeply planted in a thoroughly exemplary manner, the clematis should be watered slowly and given a liquid feed if it is planted at the start of the growing season. Then you should give the whole area a really thick, deep mulch, and to keep the snails away, surround the base with a wide swathe of sheep-poo mulch, a copper ring, or tuck in a few slug pellets (if you use them) around the stems. Then leave the plant well alone.

As the growing season advances, drench the plant every two weeks or so (depending on the weather) with 4.5 litres (1 gallon) of water, temporarily pulling away the mulch and applying it very slowly so that moisture reaches the plant's root system and doesn't just wash away over the surrounding soil. The last thing you want to do is water too little, encouraging the roots to grow upwards to the surface of the soil where they are likely to be baked in hot weather. If you think you may have been a little foolhardy in your choice of planting site, sink a plastic pot or drinks bottle (top down in the soil with its bottom cut off) adjacent to the new plant, and fill it with water a few times each week.

Shading the roots

It is surprising how many gardeners – even complete beginners – will rightly tell you that 'clematis roots should be shaded'. However, few do it adequately. I have seen so many sad little plants dried to a crisp – most of them still tied to their garden centre canes – against blisteringly sunny walls, with stems emerging from soil that looks as though it was imported from the Arizona desert, and with nothing more substantial than a couple of bits of broken terracotta flower pot placed pathetically on the ground in front of them to 'shade the roots'.

'Shading the roots' actually means planting the clematis so that it is protected from the midday sun by the foliage of other plants – preferably shrubs and preferably evergreen. If clematis are planted against sunny brick walls, which act as vast storage radiators, it means more than this. For a start, the clematis should be planted at least 45cm (18in) from the wall. 'Shading' can mean placing a large, thick paving stone over the base of the plant on top of its mulch, or it can mean placing a container of other plants in front of the clematis – a good idea, because the clematis will be 'watered' by proxy. It does mean making a big fuss, but fortunately only for the first year or two. Once clematis have got their feet firmly down under, you can be much more lackadaisical. A good, thick, foody mulch spread widely around the root area every spring should be all that is required.

Clematis wilt

Even the best efforts of the most dedicated gardener can all come to nought when, just as the plant is really getting cracking and shinning up its support at a rate of knots, one shoot after another wilts. Steadfastly ignoring all attempts to revive it with copious drinks, the poor plant hangs lifeless and blackening in the wind, finally turning up its toes and dying. The dreaded clematis wilt has struck. Or has it? Some recent research has shown that a substantial number of so-called clematis wilt deaths are, in fact, caused by slug and snail damage at the base of new plants (hence the need to buy plants with more than one emerging shoot, and the advice about slug/snail barriers at planting time).

Whatever the apparent cause of the problem, the course of action is the same: cut the plant down, make sure it is well watered and well mulched and check for slugs and snails in the vicinity. Then just wait. Whatever the cause of 'death', if the roots are sound the plant will shoot back up. Perhaps it will not be immediate, but by the end of the growing season there should definitely be signs of substantial life in the form of new strong shoots. Don't relax the slug and snail vigil.

What you absolutely must not do is dig the plant up and replace it with another one, because if the cause was clematis wilt, then the virus in the soil can transfer itself to the new plant and the whole thing could

73

happen again. If the clematis re-emerges, it will thereafter be resistant to wilt (a bit like measles in that you can only get it once). If your clematis, having recovered, keels over yet again you know it was pest damage or just plain shoddy treatment on your part in the first place.

We will leave death and destruction behind and move on to another problem for would-be clematis growers.

Support

I have already described various ways in which to support climbing plants, but I think it should be stressed that clematis do need careful treatment in the early stages if they are to perform at their best. I have also said that clematis prefer to ramble around on other plants and seem to do best this way. But however you grow them, you should put in some fairly fine-gauge support for them to latch on to for the first few feet of their growth. The bamboo cane and those loathsome green plastic ties and staples that they come with should be regarded as very temporary and should be removed as soon as suitable alternatives have been put in place and firmly grabbed. Equally loathsome, in my view, is that semi-rigid plastic mesh sold (in brown, green or white) by the metre as 'clematis support'. Chicken wire looks much better and lasts just as long.

IDENTIFYING CLEMATIS 'GROUPS'

So much for new clematis. What, now, about the ones you already have and don't really understand?

You may have noticed on their labels and in books about them, that the powers-that-be divide clematis into three broad groups which they call, helpfully for once, A, B and C, or 1, 2 and 3. They are divided thus partly because their pruning methods differ and this is supposed to simplify things for us. Understanding the broad groupings may, as well as enabling you to choose appropriate types for whatever function you wish the clematis to perform, help you to work out what to do with the ones you already may have. As with everything, there are all sorts of subdivisions and bits in brackets to make us all think we can't understand, but basically it goes like this.

Group A (or 1)

This group is made up of vigorous species and hybrids that flower on the previous season's growth from January to May the next year.

Popular examples that we have mentioned above are the rampant *Clematis montana* and *C. armandii*, plus *C. cirrhosa* var. *balearica* (the last two are evergreen). There are also some more refined and delicate ones such as *Clematis alpina* and *C. macropetala*, with small flowers and ferny leaves.

How do you prune them? It has to be said that the whoppers look best unpruned, and they should really only be grown in places where they can grow to at least 5m (16ft) in height. But if it is necessary to limit their growth and, let us be realistic, few of us have the sort of space where it would not be, you should cut off the first crop of long new shoots that are produced just as the clematis stops flowering. More long shoots will subsequently be produced, but the growth rate will have been reduced by about a third. These new shoots will carry the next year's flowers, and should therefore not be messed around with later on in the summer. Every few years it will be necessary to have a proper sort out and hack back after flowering. However hard you prune them back, they are very hard to kill.

A word of warning about *Clematis armandii*. People try to grow it in small gardens, thinking that an evergreen clematis must give unbeatable year-round value – but it does not drop its old leaves. So when it marches onwards after flowering, producing a wild array of the juiciest new growth to carry the next year's flowers, it will leave behind an ugly display of long dangly 'everbrown' leaves to delight you. The answer is to prune it quite hard, right from the first year, or to somehow weave the new shoots over the old growth and tell yourself you will 'sort it out next year'. (See also the cautionary tale on pages 79–80.)

Clematis macropetala and *C. alpina* are altogether more well behaved, and like nothing better than to be sent up small garden trees or over arches and bowers where they will stay, performing beautifully with little or no pruning at all. And they produce fluffy seed heads to boot. Perfect.

Group B (or 2)

These are the tricky beasts that get us all in a panic, the gorgeous drama queens that flower their socks off in the middle of summer – the real show-offs. In addition to their midsummer spectacular, they have a lesser production in about September, often with slightly different, single, flowers. They, like the Group A ones, flower on growth they put out during the previous year.

Examples of this group are numerous. However, most people know 'Nelly Moser', with its mauvy-pink flowers with each petal barred with a deeper pink, and 'The President', a mauvy-blue and so frilly that it looks like crêpe paper.

How do you prune them? It has to be said that the pruning of this group is complicated, and therefore usually not done at all by the timid tweakers, which is why so many gardeners, having planted these really showy clematis, end up with an ugly, unproductive bird's-nest. The bird's-nest is all the more annoying if you have grown clematis from this group among roses or shrubs that need to be pruned at a different time. It can all lead to serious lethargy in the pruning department.

What you should do is cut Group B clematis back to about 23cm (9in) from the base in the second spring after planting, to promote branching growth. I appreciate that it is well-nigh impossible to bring yourself to do this dreadful little task. After all, who in their right minds, having dug, watered, mulched, fed, fended off pests, put up chicken wire, dragged around paving stones and generally been to hell and back for the sake of one small clematis, is going to be happy to cut the whole thing down to 23cm (9in), especially when it has finally made it into the big league and is about to offer you some flowers to photograph and brag to your friends about? But this is what you have to do, and if you grit your teeth and do it, you will be rewarded, I assure you, with a chunkier and more floriferous plant ever more.

Subsequent cutting back is not nearly so heart-stopping. You just trim out dead stems and cut back by about one-third in late February, bearing in mind that if the plant is cut too dramatically at this time, early flowers will be fewer and smaller. Take great care during this early trim not to cut bits that look totally dead but actually carry substantial amounts of growth on their ends. After the plant has done its stuff, remove the dead flowers and a short length of the old flowering shoots to encourage the production of a second crop of flowers in September. What you are doing here is removing tired growth, similar to pruning early-flowering shrubs. But you also want that additional late summer crop of flowers, so your pruning is more in the order of 'trimming'. If you remove too much, you won't get the flowers.

Overgrown and neglected Group B clematis can be cut right down in the spring, but you will lose the best crop of flowers that year.

By way of encouragement, I can tell you that I cut back to ground level a very old Group B clematis completely one November. The next year it grew back and gave me a dozen or so flowers in mid- to late summer. The following spring it was absolutely, utterly wonderful. I then had to start thinning out the shoots that had flowered and doing all the text-book stuff. Much easier on a totally revamped plant, I assure you.

Group C (or 3)

These really are the most useful and accommodating of them all. They are the ones I urge all those who have had zero luck with clematis so far to rush out and buy.

They flower abundantly from July to (if you are lucky) early October on the shoots they make in the current season. There are loads to choose from, some of them really common like 'Jackmanii' (masses of deep-purple floppy flowers), and 'Perle d'Azur' (ethereal mauve/blue). There is a whole mob of smaller-flowered ones formerly called 'Viticella hybrids' (and now newly classified) that grow and flower incredibly well and have resistance to wilt, and there are some really wonderful later summer-autumn ones like Clematis orientalis, which is yellow, C. flammula and C. rehderiana, cream and scented, that give the garden a real lift when things are looking a bit dried out and drained of vigour.

How do you prune them? Oh joy, oh joy, it is simplicity itself. You can cut them to about knee-height either in late February or March. If you are growing them up trees, you can cut them back to the branch level of their hosts whence they will scramble aloft again during the summer. All of this means that you can grow them into a variety of shrubs and roses and just prune them out once a year. No more angst, no more bird's-nests.

You can actually cut them down at any time during the dormant months as long as the weather is not too frosty. Mind you, when it's *that* cold I prefer to slum into Tunbridge Wells and look at clothes shops. No danger of untimely clematis pruning around here.

To sum up. Hurrah for Group C clematis. Go to it. Grow more of them.

GOOD COMPANIONS

Here are some climbers and shrubs that work well together:

Rosa 'Mermaid' (pale yellow climbing rose) and *Clematis* 'Jackmanii Superba' (purple)

Rhamnus alaternus 'Argenteovariegata' (green and white variegated evergreen shrub, with tiny reddish buds) and *Clematis* 'Kermesina' (Vt) (deep red)

Rosa glauca (grey/purple-leaved shrub rose, with scarlet hips) and *Clematis* 'Madame Julia Correvon' (Vt) (pink/scarlet)

Rosa 'Compassion' (apricot/pink climbing rose, with gold centre) and *Lonicera* × *heckrottii* 'Gold Flame' (apricot and goldish-yellow honeysuckle)

Solanum crispum 'Glasnevin' (mauve/blue, with deep-yellow centre) and yellow annual climbing nasturtiums

Clematis 'Perle d'Azur' (ethereal mauve/blue) and *Vitis vinifera* 'Purpurea' (purple-leaved ornamental vine) – famous at Sissinghurst Castle garden

Any shrub or climbing rose with *Clematis* 'Alba Luxurians' (Vt)

Vitis coignetiae 'Claret Cloak' (reddish-leaved vine) with *Clematis* 'Madame Julia Correvon' (Vt) (pink/scarlet)

Early and late Dutch honeysuckle (*Lonicera periclymenum* 'Belgica' and *L. periclymenum* 'Serotina') grown together
Lonicera periclymenum 'Graham Thomas' (cream-yellow honeysuckle) with *Clematis* 'Perle d'Azur' (ethereal mauve/blue)

AND A FINAL THOUGHT: MISHMASH CONTROL

This chapter of perhaps humiliatingly obvious common sense is probably all very helpful if you are planting anew, or have plenty of space, but what about that appalling mishmash of too-close-for comfort climbers (usually with clematis heavily involved somewhere) to which I referred earlier? The answer is glaringly simple: decide to cut things right down, preferably remove completely the trouble-makers, and let the rest start again. I know, I know, it sounds so simple, but when you stand in your garden and look at your *Clematis montana* waving at you from the top of the neighbour's cherry tree and triffid-like branches of another neighbour's grapevine trying to strangle you as you speak, while the ground is littered with the mildewy leaves of simply everyone's so-called evergreen honeysuckle, it all just seems too much. But I promise you, if you actually take a weekend out of your life and do it, you will never regret it.

In certain circumstances, great care should be exercised – particularly when you have just acquired a new garden. I am reminded of the sad but hilarious tale told to me by a London friend. Blitzing the massed and matted climbers and overgrown shrubs on her boundary in late winter, she came across a seemingly dead limb of something massive with no sign of life on it anywhere. Having been told by me to overcome her wimpish tendencies where pruning was concerned at all costs, she cut. It was such a massive thing she was forced to fetch the pruning saw. Two doors down the road, the 'owners' of a *Clematis armandii* in full, heavenly flower were stunned when the whole thing wilted for no apparent reason.

Generally, though, hard pruning never hurt anyone, or anything. I am sure the aforementioned *Clematis armandii* did not die, and that it leapt back into life in its real owner's garden, for a while, anyway, until it got the wanderlust again. There are certainly times when brutal and radical first-aid pruning is absolutely unavoidable. Once upon a time, in another garden and another life, it nearly broke my heart to cut down an ancient *Clematis montana* sprawling up the back of my house a matter of days before it opened its flowers, just because of some builders. It was back up there, flowering again a year later, unstoppable, looking stunning.

CHAPTER 5

A few thoughts on mixed borders

I have always considered the words 'mixed border' quite grand and intimidating, and I even find myself using a Lady Bracknell voice just thinking about them. It has to be said that most of us don't have 'mixed borders' in the proper sense. What many of us settle for can best be described as a 'mixed strip', generally along one or more sides of our gardens, where favoured flowering plants flourish – or if we are a bit slack or don't know what we are doing, fail, flop over or run amok. Invariably, there are parts of these borders that are embarrassingly gappy at important times of year, as well as in the winter, of course, and the whole thing is never, ever, quite satisfactory.

Perhaps, you might argue, I should spend my time and effort persuading readers to try something new, something a little more 'now'. How about swathes of immaculate gravel – all clean lines, with just a hint of Japan and the odd minimalist container? Or should I encourage you to waft around trying to make an arty wild-flower mess or strive over acres of echinaceas and go for a transatlantic prairie fandango? Or would you prefer to be encouraged to create gardens that look like post-2012 Olympics traffic roundabouts, with hairy-hoary massed grasses punctuated by a few sedums and the odd skeletal perovskia?

I would be wasting my time if I tried, however, since imported garden fashions come and go (witness the speed with which Antipodean decking slipped in and slid out again), and the small plots of land behind or around the majority of rather ordinary houses in Britain lend themselves, by and large, to the old ways – the paths to the shed, the bit of grass, the borders. And surprisingly enough, most of us seem to be rather conventional, too.

By the same token that most people (especially men) think that a lawn is an important and essential part of their gardens, most people (especially women) hanker after an area of harmonious planting in which to nurture and tend the plants they love, in other words a mixed border of some kind, with perhaps a few veg and herbs thrown in as well for good measure. We may play around with gravel and spiky plants, bog gardens or bits of wild-ery here and there when we have space, but the need for a decent 'border' has been planted deeply in the British gardening psyche. It is what this nation of gardeners is apparently admired for, so most of us just enjoy fiddling away, trying to 'get it right' – and getting better at it all the time.

What is a real mixed border?

What exactly is it that we hanker after? The mixed border is the natural successor to the herbaceous borders of the gardening era when labour was cheap, gardens were large and it was acceptable for the wealthy to show off. Truly herbaceous borders – those composed entirely of plants that die right back in the winter – are few and far between these days. I remember as a small child (brought up with a tiny garden that was then home to rabbits and bantam hens, but with a large nearby allotment), being amazed at a display of towering delphiniums in a huge old-fashioned herbaceous border at Bristol Zoo. To a six-year-old, they seemed taller and more magnificent than the elephants I had been taken to see, and I suppose that was the point of them: size and splendour, if only for a few short weeks of the year. We tend to demand more, and less, of our smaller gardens now. For a start, we want to look at something for the whole year, not just high summer. And most of us baulk at all the hard work that growing so much herbaceous stuff involves.

So the mixed border, in its proper form, is quite unashamedly a bit of this and a bit of that. It is a mixture of roses, flowering and foliage shrubs, both evergreen and deciduous, to give it some kind of permanent backbone. In among these are bulbs, biennials, a fair number of herbaceous perennials, and a few annuals thrown in for good measure (to fill up the gaps or add a bit of seasonal oomph). As the word border implies, the whole thing is set against a backdrop of a hedge, a fence or a wall, most probably with climbing plants on it as well. The real skill is sorting everything out so that it is relatively easy to service and maintain, and that things happen all over the place for as much of the year as possible. Alas, it takes time, patience and a lot of plant knowledge to really get it right.

There are wonderful examples of mixed borders in most of the major gardens in Britain, but these grand borders with their huge depth and enormous swathes of colour can seem all too daunting and irrelevant to the owners of small gardens. Indeed, you can well be put off the whole thing for ever as you realise, for example, that the amount of ground covered by pink phlox alone in the famous Long Border at Great Dixter is just about equal to the entire square footage of your own (so-called) border. Purists will tell you that you just can't do it on a small scale and that small borders look 'spotty' (a favourite put-down of the horticulturally challenged by the spatially privileged). However, in my view it is part of the on-going challenge that is real gardening: the annual keeping-the-fingers-crossed cliff-hanger to see if this year's wheezes work the way you want them to.

A moving feast

It is undoubtedly true that achieving a half-way decent patch of garden that you can call a mixed border without blushing is extremely hard in a small space and it takes time (a couple of years at the very least) to look established. If and when you do get it 'right', you will probably have changed your taste or gardening style and discovered a whole new lot of plants you simply must have. So the enterprise has to be seen as a constantly moving feast, a never-ending game. It is not for those seeking an easy gardening life.

Even I have to admit that it is actually advisable for the owners of small borders to give up gardening altogether in the deepest, dreariest winter months. This is the time of year when owners of large borders bore the pants off you with tales of hoar frost on their herbaceous perennials or the ravishing red stems of their three square yards of cornus caught magically in the slanting winter sunlight. 'Small borderers' miss out on all that for obvious reasons, and anyway it sometimes gets too cold on February mornings to think about venturing outside for the customary recce *en pyjama*. It is far more fun at this time of year to spend any designated gardening time sitting with your feet up leafing through bulb catalogues and old gardening magazines to give your fantasies a run for their money.

WHERE DO YOU START?

I will approach borders from two directions. First, how do you tart up an old and boring one that doesn't work for you, and second, how do you make a new one out of virgin ground? In both cases the first move involves winning a battle for extra space, since I assume that as a gardening obsessive you are angling for a bigger slice of the garden pie in which to spread your horticultural wings (how about that for mixing three leisure-oriented metaphors?). This generally involves either pinching a bit of treasured lawn from a grassaholic, or banishing footballs, or confining children's ghastly plastic play rubbish to an invisible area under a dripping, aphid-infested lime tree where nothing grows. None of these feats is easily achieved, as we all know.

I should say at this point that this book deliberately does not set out to give definite design advice. I am a dedicated graduate of the well-known sticks-and-string school of garden design, preferring to let gardens develop around my passion for plants rather than spend my time trying to tone down what can so easily become a runaway fantasy in bricks, paving and sawn timber (which often happens if you start using graph paper).

I realise that I am extremely fortunate in that I have always been able to visualise what I want a garden to look like and, over time, have learnt how to achieve the 'look' by teaching myself what works where in the garden. I have taken a lot of stick from professional garden designers, many of whom provide a missing link for their clients, mapping out for them a new shape for their garden that they cannot themselves 'see'. But, should you employ a designer, try to make sure that they do not stuff your garden full of plants that are, essentially, their choice. If you are at all interested in growing things, the real gardening begins once the designers and builders have left, as you personalise your garden and make it a place where you can fiddle around, make a few mistakes, but above all enjoy the plants that really please you. You need to understand what goes on out there, or your investment in the design can become a source of stress and anxiety, which is absolutely what gardening should not be.

And I will put down another marker here. Try not to get too fixated, in the early days, on creating borders of harmonious colour. The gardening world has always been divided: is this thing we love art, or is it science? The answer is, I strongly believe, if you get the simple science right – learn how to grow plants successfully, learn what makes them tick (or tick badly or even stop ticking), you can fiddle about with colour harmony and leaf contrasts – all the arty stuff – far more easily and with greater confidence and satisfaction. End of sermon.

OLD BORDERS

First, size

Most of the 'wannabe' borders I have seen are just too small and mean to deserve the name. To get anything like a satisfying depth of planting, they need to be at the very least 1.5m (5ft) deep at some point and about 2.5m (8ft) long. This may seem unrealistically ambitious for a small garden, but can often be achieved by taking the planting area across one or more corners. Most of our gardens are square or rectangular, and such borders that exist are frequently just strips along the edges. By extending the planting area boldly across a corner, you not only achieve a greater depth, you distract the eye from the real shape of the garden which instantly adds interest.

Second, site

Logically, it makes sense to have your main border set away from the house, where you can see it from a good vantage point, usually from the kitchen sink, but, if you are lucky, from your living room window or terrace. Having decided on the best amendment to the shape of the border, you then have to consider which way it faces, because you need to work out how much light it will get and for how many months of the year. It is really important that you take this into consideration since it affects which plants will be happy there.

If the best site for your border happens to be in a north-facing corner, for example, don't despair. Happy, well-grown, shade-loving plants look splendid; you can go for big, bold, shiny leaves and ferns, for example, enlivened by variegated evergreens and a few tall white-flowered plants such as Japanese anemones, foxgloves or tobacco plants. The secret is to plant things that will grow well, rather than to hammer away with plants that need more light than you can provide, and that will never perform satisfactorily without it. I have explained more about the different types of light and shade in the chapter on shrubs (see pages 39–40), and these guidelines apply to all plants, not just shrubs.

Third, timing

The accepted time to do major things to your border is either October/November or about March. However, I find that if you get really fed up with your garden, a good time to start blitzing it is September. Most gardens are a bit shot by then. Our memory of what looked good and what looked awful is fresh, the weather is pleasant enough to work, children are back at school or wherever, and energy levels generally are high. You can still get herbaceous perennials at most garden centres and nurseries, some still with flowers on that will help you with your border planning. Furthermore, if you manage to get new things planted and old things replanted at this time, they may have a month or so to establish themselves in their new sites before the soil and the weather cool down.

You may have to take a little extra care, making sure that the plants are watered in well, but in my view the benefits more than compensate for the extra work needed.

What about existing plants?

Once you accept the limitations of the aspect of your potential revamped border, you then have to take a good, long and, if necessary, ruthless look at the plants already growing in the area, to see if they fit into the new scheme of things. The most common problem I encounter is that even knowledgeable and otherwise sensible gardeners will hang on to plants, particularly roses and huge clumps of non-flowering irises or peonies just because they are there. On countless occasions, I have been asked to help reorganise a border and been told by the owner, in a tired and exasperated voice, that the stringy rose at the back just happened to get left there because when they moved into the house it was the only plant in the entire garden that was in flower and that they recognised.

The joke is that I have done this myself. I left a rich crimson rose in a key position in a softly coloured border in my old garden in Wandsworth in London. I started off by apologising for its presence in my otherwise tasteful border – it fortunately only had two major flushes of flower each season and I could hardly deadhead it soon enough. In the end, as the fashion for bolder colour schemes began to take hold, people started to tell me what a wonderful eye-catching statement the rose made. I nodded sagely every time (tongue firmly in cheek), shamelessly letting people believe that the rose was there intentionally. But I learnt my lesson. Two gardens later, moving into a small jungle in a Sussex village, I had tough decisions to take and, I am proud to say, I took my own stern advice – removing a mass of plants, including shrubs, that were not of my choosing – and have never regretted it.

Keep or clear?
Large, immovable shrubs that you definitely want to keep and that are in by chance absolutely the right place can be left in situ. You can simply

build your new border around them. But you should certainly think twice about keeping late-flowering whoppers like *Buddleja davidii* or lavatera in a small mixed border. They need such drastic pruning each spring to keep them in bounds that their presence makes it difficult to keep the border looking balanced, and obviously limits the number of other plants that will cope with the lack of elbow room in the border in late summer.

Other plants, including herbaceous perennials, some biennial seedlings (foxgloves, honesty, forget-me-nots and so on) and whatever bulbs you unearth should be removed completely and re-sited temporarily in another part of the garden designated a 'nursery bed'. Or temporarily potted. You should put labels with each plant, even with rough descriptions of the plants as you remember them since, although this decampment is only relatively short term, it is amazing how quickly you forget what things are.

If your garden upheaval is not very large, there is no point in going to the trouble of creating a proper nursery bed. You can get away with spreading a sheet of plastic on the lawn or terrace, dumping on it the plants that you want to keep (with labels), covering all the roots with newspaper and wetting the whole area with a hose. As long as the plant roots are not exposed to sun and wind, and the newspaper remains moist, they should survive for a week or so.

Transplanting existing shrubs

As often as not, there will be shrubs you want to keep that are definitely in the wrong place, and it really is worth having a go at transplanting them. Roses hate to be disturbed when they are in leaf or flower, and may just drop everything or even die if you try moving them. They will occasionally recover but, if you love them, it is not worth taking the risk. It might be better to wait until they are virtually leafless in November before undertaking the work in the border. Remember, shrubs, even person-sized ones, can be moved if it is really unavoidable. Some of them absolutely loathe root disturbance of any kind, and will let you know by wilting alarmingly for weeks. Worse, they may give up the ghost. Notable sulkers are the evergreens, so try to move them during dull and windless weather, while large shrubby euphorbias and mature cistus behave even worse. But it is always worth having a go at transplanting things since it is better to have a stab at it than to chuck them out without a fight. Like a lot of gardening, it is all common sense really, but then, time and time again, common sense deserts obsessives. Guidelines for moving shrubs are included in the earlier chapter on shrubs (see pages 50–1).

Improving the soil

Once you have cleared out all the plants you want to reinstate in the new improved border, isolated the shrubs and roses you want to keep where they are and moved or thrown out the others, you can start to improve the soil with organic matter. There is more information about the need for this in the earlier chapter on soil.

I do recommend that you don't skimp on the amount of chunky organic stuff that you add to the soil before you plant up your border, be it well-rotted horse manure, mushroom compost, home-made compost, composted bark or some such 'soil improver'. Organic stuff plumps up and improves all soils, whether it is thick and clay-like or light and sandy, or something in between. Your plants will get a really good start and you will not need to think about adding any more, except as a mulch perhaps, for a year or even two. As a rough guide, you should reckon on digging in at least a bucketful, preferably two, of stuff plus, if you like, a roughly sprinkled handful of bonemeal or other phosphate per bucket into each square metre. Your plant roots will really appreciate it. If your soil is ropey use more.

At the same time as forking the stuff in, you will have the chance to weed properly, removing any spaghetti-like roots that are the hallmarks of troublesome perennial invasive customers such as bindweed and ground elder, and trying to get out whole the deep taproots of dandelions. By digging, you are bound to bring a lot of dormant weed seeds to the surface of the soil so you should not be deceived by the fact that you appear to have done a thorough job. You won't have, with just one go at it, but that shouldn't stop you trying, particularly with the aforementioned nasties.

Once you have done all this preparation, you can start on the really interesting bit – planning things out and shopping. But first I should, as I explained, approach border preparation from the other direction.

COMPLETELY NEW BORDERS IN VIRGIN GROUND

As I have already said, new borders are generally created after often tricky negotiations with other interested parties about priorities in the garden. Be tough. It may be worth mentioning here that in my view there is no sense in trying to have anything other than a row of sad and battered-looking climbers in a mean strip a couple of feet wide grudgingly sliced off the side of a football pitch.

Removing turf and then digging it into the soil before you plant so that it rots down underneath everything is an excellent way to make sure a new border is well fed. If you are making a border in a patch of former lawn, therefore, you should remove the grass in strips, cutting it first into rectangles that you can slip your spade under – a bit like carving up flapjacks in a tin. This is a back-breaking job, made even harder if you are, like me in my old huge garden, daft enough to try to remove what felt at the time like the entire surface of the globe on a very hot day when the lawn was rock hard and parched.

It helps a lot, I subsequently found out, if you wait until the ground is moist and if you can borrow a special long-handled flat-bladed spade called a turfing iron. If you can't get hold of one of these, just soldier on with an ordinary spade, but take it slowly. Aim to take off a layer about 5cm (2in) deep of the grass and as much of its roots as possible. If the grass is in good condition and not too full of weeds, save the best bits for patching other bald areas or repairing the collapsed edges of the lawn. You will get better at removing the turf in a more orderly and regular way as you progress, so it makes sense (if you do want to save some for patching) to start with the worst area of grass first. Stack all the bits somewhere close by, because you will be digging them back in upside down shortly.

Trench digging

This is such a worthwhile thing to do before planting up a new border. It is a nightmare job it is true, but one which you can boast about for years as you watch your plants flourish. Basically what you do is divide your area into rectangles in your mind's eye, and tackle each rectangle of ground in turn.

1 Starting, as it were, at the top right-hand corner of a rectangle, dig a trench across it at least a spade's depth deep, putting the soil you remove on a plastic sheet or in a barrow that you can drag or wheel to the other end of the plot. To dig efficiently and get a good rhythm going in what will inevitably be fairly compacted soil, jab your spade downwards vertically at right angles to your cutting line before removing each spadeful, so that each clod comes out in a manageable squarish chunk. Assuming you are reclaiming a former lawn, the next step is to place strips of the old turf face down in the bottom of the trench and sprinkle a handful of bonemeal or general fertiliser for each linear yard of trench on top of the turf.

2 Then go back to the beginning of the trench, step backwards and dig another trench, turning the contents over as you dump it on top of the upside-down turf in the first trench. Chop away at the soil to break up the clods. As you do this you may well see bits of dandelion root or other perennial weeds that got left behind during the turf-cutting operation, and these should be removed in case they sprout later. By putting the turf in upside down, you are minimising the risk of it coming back up through your borders, but you should make sure that your trenches are deep enough not to let the grass get any silly ideas.

3 Work over the entire border area, finally putting the contents of

the first trench on top of the turf and fertiliser in the last trench. If you run out of turf (we all know that these things never work out the way they say in books) or if you're working on bare soil, put a 10cm (4in) layer of mushroom compost, rotted horse manure or any other organic stuff you can find in the bottom of the trenches.

Every so often, put your spade down, straighten up your spine, put your hands flat in the small of your back and gently stretch backwards, then roll your shoulders around. It all helps ease the strain.

At the end of the process you can stand back and feel so, so pleased with yourself. Then go and have a hot, smug bath.

Of course, not everyone has the time, the strength or the inclination to trench-dig their gardens, and it really is not the end of the world if you don't. Furthermore, you will always find the odd (generally organic) gardener who says that so much disturbance to the soil is actually a bad thing. So if, for whatever reason, it suits you better not to go the whole hog, then you can just dump as much organic stuff as you can muster in an even layer over the soil and fork it in as deeply as you can, removing any weeds as you go, at the same time adding, if you feel inclined, a sprinkling of a balanced granular fertiliser or chicken manure. You, too, will qualify for the deep, hot, smug bath after this.

Whatever you do in the way of digging, try to leave the area to settle – give the worms time to calm down before you start to plant. Find something else to get on with for about a fortnight or more, if you can bear it.

PLANNING A BORDER

This is, quite frankly, one of the bits of this book that I dreaded writing originally, and the years that have passed since I did so have not made it any easier to revise. I still don't know how anyone ever constructively advises others on how to plant up a border, since I am sure everyone just fiddles about in their own way and finally gets there, or gives it up and takes up ballroom dancing. All I can offer are bits of rather mundane-sounding practical advice, when what people really want to get from you is a magic formula, a foolproof verbal planting plan.

The best description I ever read about how to go about border planning was written years ago by the late Christopher Lloyd. Presumably it struck a chord because it was so close to what I have tried to do, and explain, in the past. It was reassuring to find that he didn't mention drawing things out precisely to scale with perfect little coloured circles to indicate different plants, all in a meticulous, organised, tablets-of-stone sort of way. So it is without shame that I shall, with personal additions, subtractions and amendments, try to recall the gist of what he advised.

I've got a little list...

It is best if you make lists and then do some sort of blobby bird's-eye view drawing before you even think of going shopping, and before you plant or replant a single thing. Even before that, however, list all of the plants you simply must have. This list will have on it things you have fallen for in other people's gardens, things you remember from childhood, things you couldn't imagine living without. To this list, add the plants that you already have, know and understand and that you really want to keep (these are the ones in the 'nursery bed' or under the wet newspaper, remember?).

How to divide up your lists
When making lists you must consider the growing requirements of the plants you want; I am sure I have gone on enough about sun, shade,

93

moisture and general soil conditions and so on for you to realise that these things are of vital importance. There are, however, other considerations that are just as crucial: you need also to think of the flowering season of plants as well as their eventual heights. It is the gradual mastery of all this that, I hate to say it, turns enthusiastic and spontaneous spendthrifts into competent, respected and genuine gardeners with EotN (Envy of the Neighbourhood) borders. Learning how to get things growing well in the 'right' places is more important than the complexities of colour. I will have another go at this theory later in the chapter.

When I was starting out I found it helpful to organise my lists quite carefully. I would make a 'shade' list and a 'sun' list, and divide each into 'front row', 'middle' and 'back', according to their flowering heights, and also make a note of their months or weeks of interest and whether they were annuals, biennials or perennials – ticking off those plants that I already had, so that gradually a 'shopping list' could be made. It sounds a lot more organised than I am by nature, but it really was worth thinking about plants in this way, in my opinion. At least I had a way of ensuring that everything in the border didn't burst into activity at the same time and all in one place, with huge rapacious things completely masking the more subtle tiddlers.

It is with sinking heart, however, that having brought you to this place, I am now going to more or less abandon you. The original version of this book contained an entire section listing my then-favourite plants set out this way, intending to help by way of example. But when I came to review everything, the plants I had used then seem now to be rather banal (my own knowledge of and taste in plants has unsurprisingly progressed and changed a lot in the decade since I wrote the original). Furthermore, the lack of illustrations made the lists unappealing reading. So rather than update the plants – I ditched the entire section.

So when you are a bit foxed and need to find, just as an example, a shade-tolerant perennial that will flower in late summer at about 1m (3ft) high to fill a space at the back of the border (oh, alright then, how about Japanese anemones? Or if the patch gets some summer sun, even a tall white phlox, *Phlox paniculata* 'David'...), I am leaving you in the hands of those who write illustrated comprehensive plant directories and to the internet (the online Plant Selector on the RHS website, for example, and frequently updated apps such as The Garden Mentor). By the time you get to making your blobby bird's-eye-view drawing (more of this later in the chapter), and eventually planting up your border, you will have a much better chance of getting things right. The sought-after EotN status may well be around the corner, but at least you will have thought about plants in a useful way, and made it less likely that you will have planted things that really, really won't work, just because you like them. And having said all that, I am still capable of having the odd rush of blood to the head and getting it wrong – even after years of trying not to.

Beware of friends bearing gifts

I would add at this point that in my experience one should be very, very careful about being offered a load of dross by well-meaning and sympathetic friends, who, on seeing all that naked soil will, at the drop of a hat, treat your garden like a horticultural land-fill site, dumping on you all the overgrown and unruly hooligans from their own overstuffed borders. These are probably plants, incidentally, that they themselves unwittingly accepted in the same circumstances years earlier.

So keep quiet about your new border, or you will find endless 'gifts' of *Leucanthemum maximum*, anonymous watery orange oriental poppies and alstroemerias, *Sisyrinchium striatum* (the green-leaved self-seeder), yellow loosestrife, *Geranium* 'Claridge Druce', lemon balm and numerous others lovingly pressed into your eager soily hands. Each plant is pleasant enough in its way and in the right context (actually, I think I may be fibbing here), but none is the sort of unruly guest you want at your own party, if you know what I mean. By all means beg and wheedle shamelessly for things you really want – that is what we all do. But remember you are in charge. Not your mother or your mother-in-law, not your best gardening friend, not your next door neighbour – not anyone. This is your baby. You haven't a hope in hell of getting things right for yourself if you go all weak at the knees and are grateful for any old cast-offs.

Hidden paths

Back to the border. First, the nuts and bolts bit. If you have a decent depth to the border, make a path – it need only be a narrow strip with bark chippings on it or some stepping stones – from which to service the back of it. It may seem like a waste of precious planting space, but you will regret it if you don't put it in at the start, and it will soon be virtually hidden as things grow so that only you will know where you can tread. In my former gardens I ignored this important piece of advice that I used to hand out with such aplomb (do as I say, not as I do). I seemed to spend my life during the summer teetering painfully on one cramped leg trying not to snap the delphiniums off while I wrestled with the climbers from next door that were trying to muscle in on the act, as I tried to twist my body so I could deadhead all around me. Daft. I am much more grown up now, I hasten to say. Paths simply everywhere and climbers properly catered for.

Start at the back

Get your back row of climbers sorted out, making sure before you plant them that they have adequate support – or they will yawn forward on to all your other new plants. Remember that if you have a hedge or plants that need mid-season pruning and tweaking, you need to be able to get to them somehow. Some borders – especially in small gardens where you are often trying to distract the eye from a less than lovely view of the neighbouring buildings – look good if they contain a big show-off plant. Current fashion may well steer you towards a spiky thing – a phormium, perhaps, or, if your garden is sheltered, a cordyline. Or it could be a bit of rounded or pointed evergreen blobbery, like a clipped box bush, or something that isn't a plant at all, such as a sundial or an urn. Whatever it is, it will provide you with your foundation stone, from which you build your border outwards.

Next turn your attention to any shrubs you want to include. I think they look better in a harmonising group of two or three if there is space. Ideally, each member of the group should do its thing at a different time of the year, or have a strong contrast in leaf shape or colour with its neighbour. Don't forget about the bleak winter months completely; make sure that you include evergreens, preferably ones that also flower well. When it comes to deciding where they should be placed, don't, however, plant them where they will block the view of the rest of your border from your best vantage point. Or where they will steal the thunder, as it were, from any deliberately eye-catching feature described above.

If you simply must have roses in your border, remember you cannot plant a new rose in the place of an old one without changing the soil (more of this, and the use of beneficial mycorrhizal fungi in the chapter on soil, see page 22). Also, remember that gorgeous old shrub roses are quite hard to accommodate in smaller borders because they flower for such a short time and have such wide-spreading shapes. Look instead at some of the English roses, Hybrid Perpetual or Modern Shrub roses, which flower for longer and some of which (such as 'Ballerina') are smaller or work well as standards at the back of the border to give height.

I could go on, with various sensible and mumsy utterings about the importance of autumn leaf colour, shrubs with berries or coloured stems for winter – but it is exactly the sort of smug stuff in gardening books that I have always found so irritating. What you want is chapter and verse, and all I would be giving you is the address of the library! Just remember, it is your taste, not mine or anyone else's, that is important. All I can do is help you to think in the right way, but I will give you an example or two of shrub groups in borders that have worked for me in the past.

SOME IDEAS TO CHEW OVER

Evergreens for backbone and a rounded shape: *Choisya ternata*, *Pittosporum* 'Irene Paterson' (marble variegation) or *P.* 'Tom Thumb' (small, with plum-coloured leaves)

Tall evergreens to hide a fence (in a spot with limited sun): *Viburnum tinus* and *Rhamnus alaternus* 'Argenteovariegata' (with late-flowering *Clematis* 'Kermesina' (Vt) struggling through both)

Evergreen flowering shrubs for a hot sunny site: *Phlomis fruticosa* and *Cistus* x *purpureus* (with very tall deciduous *Argyrocytisus battandieri* and *Berberis thunbergii* and a semi-evergreen weeping bamboo, *Fargesia murielae*, behind, making in all a thick, deep, fence-hiding bank of shrubs)

Getting it down on paper

Once you have decided on all this, you ought to try to do the blobby drawing on a large sheet of paper. It doesn't have to be done to scale but you should try to make the proportions of the bed look about right, and have a rough idea of the actual length and depth of the new border by pacing it out (a slightly extended female stride equals about a metre).

Start with your 'foundation stone' plant and find something from your list that would look good with it. Draw little cloud-shaped dollops on the page for each plant and put the name in each. Individual things like foxgloves that you may well want to plant in groups you can mark with crosses. Tick things off from your list as you go, and gradually build outwards in all directions, thinking all the time how things would look with their intended neighbours. Incorporate some of the 'must have' combinations of plants that you will doubtless have filed away in your brain as a result of ogling other people's borders. If your border is not going to have a focal point as such, start at one corner or a prominent place with a fairly large patch of something eye-catching, and work your way outwards from there.

Plan to leave plenty of space around shrubs; they are going to grow like the wind because of the enriched soil. Aim to put annuals next to them, or even biennials or bulbs, but don't make them fight it out with precious young perennials. The shrubs will probably win and you will have wasted time and money.

Planting in groups

Advice that you simply must plant in odd numbers with about 60cm (2ft) of space between each item is a bit hard to take when you have a small garden and there are so many things you want to try out. But, if the budget will allow and there is sufficient space, do plan to plant groups of things rather than use singletons. What you do should depend on the size of the plants in question, and the amount of space available.

It always pays to do a bit of homework before you acquire plants you are not sure about. A friend, a true horticultural innocent clearly under the influence of someone with a garden far larger than her own 15m by 9m (50ft by 30ft) patch, once bought three young plants of *Crambe cordifolia* (ultimately vast, really vast, perennials). She planted them 60cm (2ft) apart in the middle of a border no more than 3m (10ft) long and 1.2m (4ft) wide, together with other plants, none of them small. Fortunately the crambe all died.

While you can plant bigger things like acanthus – or crambe – as a single plant (and it will make a decent-sized statement from the start), the smaller perennials will get lost in singles. You could always do what I do – it works in the short term: plant two of the same thing quite close together to make a bigger single clump that you can then divide after a year – do a swap with a friend or heave something else out of the border that doesn't work in order to create more space. I did warn you that this border thing was a movable feast.

If you are lucky enough to have loads of space, you can plant perennials in great interlocking swathes, known to posh gardeners as 'drifts'. I do think posh gardeners are funny. You never hear them talk about 'drifts' of ground elder or stinging nettles, do you?

All the time you are 'weaving' your tapestry on paper and ticking things off your lists, think about not only what goes well with what, but consider what happens to each plant and when, so that you don't get all the action going on in only one part of the border at a time.

Leave colour to nature

There is a lot to think about, so my advice, as I have stated earlier, is that the last thing you should think about is colour. Unless you are blessed with a superhuman colour sense, this is the straw that can break the camel's back and get you completely bogged down. I have always maintained that colour is the last thing you should try to get right, and not the first, since this is where a lot of people go wrong. At the end of the day, plants are part of nature, and nature rarely jars the colour senses. While it is easy to be swayed by colour 'fashions' in gardening, I think you need to get your plants up and running – growing well – and once you are confident about them you can start reshuffling the pack, as it were, to get the colours right for you. That is how I learnt, anyway.

I will, however, say one or two more things on the subject of colour that may be helpful. While I think that colour-themed borders are a bit of a cop-out, there is much to be said for the addition of white in a new, otherwise colour-chaotic border. It separates things out and calms things down. I have already extolled the virtues of white foxgloves and white Japanese anemones and others, but there is a white-flowered, lime-green leaved plant that I find immensely useful in a new border to give a nice pillowy overall look, and that is common-or-garden golden-leaved feverfew. And even if it self-seeds in a rather thuggish way – plenty of gardeners think of it as a weed – you can recognise the seedlings at a glance, since they are so bright, and simply get rid of them when they are tiny. Another similar self-seeding thug/god-send for a young border is the lofty plum-leaved red orach. I rather like having these two as more or less permanent, but easily controllable members of my garden mafia. It means that there need never be any major gaps. This is hardly what you call sophisticated gardening, but there you go.

SHOPPING AND PLANTING – AT LAST

Hopefully, you will find most of the plants you want at local garden centres and nurseries. Use of both the internet and the trusty old-fashioned phone save time and money and cut down on the sort of impulse-buying that can so easily put the cat among the pigeons.

Whatever you do, don't start planting until you have at least three-quarters of the things you want to plant. For the ones you can't get hold of, you will have to make up sticks that are approximately the appropriate height, with labels on them. 'Plant' these sticks as reminders until such time as you can get the plants themselves. As a last resort, you may have to find substitutes.

First consult your 'plan', and place your new plants, still in their pots, where you intend them to go. Don't move your nursery plants or transplant from under the newspaper till the last possible moment – there is probably still quite a lot of shuffling things around to do and they won't like the wait with their roots high and dry. Do try your very best not to plant things too close together in the mistaken hope that the border will establish itself more quickly the more plants you put in. Remember that new borders *always* look naked and awful, if they are properly planted. If you get desperate, you can always add a few annuals in the first growing season – although you should watch out in case they get too big in the rich soil you have created and start cramping the style of the permanent plants.

If you have done your homework, you will have a fair idea about (eventual) relative sizes of plants, but don't be too boring about it. A few taller, slim or wafty plants towards the front of the border add a bit of necessary *je ne sais quoi* and stop the planting looking unnaturally regimented. Although this is rather a sophisticated piece of advice to give a first-time mixed borderer, it is a useful concept, I feel. If all else fails, you can trot it out in the presence of bemused acquaintances

101

to justify any 'sore thumb' mistakes that appear a few months down the line.

When you are reasonably sure of where things are going to go, plant them. Make sure that the roots of all the new plants are nice and damp. I generally soak them in a bucket of water with something like a seaweed-based 'plant growth stimulant' in it, just to give them a boost. If you have done your soil preparation properly you don't really need to add any more goodies to the soil. However, when the weather is very warm and the soil dry, water each plant into its hole before you earth it up and firm it down, but don't water thereafter for a week or so. It is worth remembering that the dry soil on the surface, surprisingly enough, holds in the moisture down below. This is why experienced gardeners never fiddle with the soil surface during a drought – it makes matters worse.

If you are both dedicated and energetic, you could apply an organic mulch of composted bark, or similar, over the entire border. I don't like using coarse bark chippings as a general mulch as the blackbirds play very messy games of football with it on the lawn. To be effective (that is, to smother emerging weed seedlings and retain moisture properly) a mulch has to be at least 8cm (3in) thick, which means you need an awful lot of organic stuff. The downside to applying an all-over mulch – in addition to the sheer amount of hard work involved – is that if you do want to change the planting or move anything around, you have to scrape it all away and you end up 'losing' it.

NOW WHAT?

You are unlikely to have got things right first time. Some things will work, others won't, and some things will take a lot longer to establish themselves than others and you will change your mind about what you are trying to achieve anyway. You can make minor adjustments before the first growing season really kicks in, but then stop and let things develop for a while. You should try to resist the temptation to play chess with your new plants all the time. I know plenty of keen-as-mustard gardeners who are absolutely hopeless in this department and nothing ever seems to get going. However, there are three things that simply must be addressed even in the first growing season of a new border, the first two of which very rarely are: Chelsea chopping, staking, deadheading and if necessary, watering.

The (absolutely not compulsory for the faint-hearted or for out-and-out beginners) Chelsea chop

The Chelsea chop is the name given to a technique carried out on some herbaceous plants, the timing of it roughly coinciding with the date in mid- to late May, of the flower show. Some herbaceous plants – those that might be over-tall or over-floppy, are improved by having their stems roughly halved in height, just as they are about to produce their flower buds. Within weeks they produce numerous flowering side shoots, and will flower prolifically, later (and on shorter stems) than they would do if left un-chopped. You can cut all the stems, half of the stems, just the front of a plant or just the back – it is a way of manipulating your border performance quite precisely once you get the hang of it. Phlox, big late-flowering daisies and sedums are all good candidates, but your author puts this information in here so that you know what other more experienced gardeners are talking about when they rabbit on about the Chelsea chop, and does not necessarily encourage inexperienced gardeners to sally forth in their pyjamas armed with a pair of shears to hack at a brand new border.

Staking

When you look at a 'grand' border in full sail in June and July, you can't really see all the hard work that went into it as little as a month earlier. The plants just stand there in all their glory. Underneath, holding it all erect so that gusts of wind or thunderstorms make little impression on it, is an absolute mass of stuff. The whole border is usually wearing the equivalent of a whalebone corset. Next time you look at a grand border put your hand in among the foliage, and you will feel it. It is all very ingenious.

The best way of supporting all sorts of herbaceous plants – the soft-stemmed ones that need the powerful undergarments – is undoubtedly to stick twigs (generally called 'pea sticks') around the individual clumps as they grow, so that they actually come up through them and are supported virtually invisibly by them for the whole season. Some gardeners weave hazel and willow into wondrous structures that are works of art in themselves. If you visit a grand garden border in May you can see how it is all done.

The cane and twine trick

In towns, it is hard to get hold of such things as hazel twigs in great quantities, so you have to resort to other methods, the easiest and cheapest of which is to use traditional bamboo canes and garden twine. You should insert at least four canes around each plant clump, each leaning at a slight outwards angle, tying one end of a piece of twine to one cane using a clove hitch, then looping it around the other canes in the group and across the circle to and fro if it is a big plant, before tying the two ends of twine together to make a firm web-like support through which the plant can grow. There are of course numerous rather pricey wire, steel and rusty iron plant supports on the market, and over time you will no doubt, like me, collect a vast array of them – hoops, grids and all sorts of horses for courses that will accommodate a variety of different types of border plants and also cut down the amount of time you have to grovel around with sticks and string.

Plants, such as delphiniums, that grow with heavy spires of flowers should ideally have a cane inserted for each flower spike, and they should then be tied laboriously to the cane as they grow. If you use the cane and web of string or a metal grid, the heavy head of the flower spike invariably breaks off in a rainstorm in the middle of June.

Trial and error

You soon get the hang of staking plants by trial and error. Paeonies, for example, positively need ultra-expensive wire mesh supports to hold their heads up for the few days that they flower – yet another reason not to grow paeonies, with which so many people are so irrationally besotted. Not many people go to the trouble of supporting herbaceous geraniums ('Johnson's Blue', 'Wargrave Pink', 'Mrs Kendall Clark' and others) but they look a million dollars if you do, and even pansies appreciate a leg-up with some low twiggy sticks and may well sprawl on upwards into neighbours in a very acceptable way.

Should you develop a passion for plants of grand operatic proportions, it doesn't necessarily mean that you have to also go into the scaffolding business. That Pavarotti among perennials, the giant thistle-like cardoon, seems to hang in there without support. If limbs happen to lean – probably because of less than full sunlight – amputation is probably the only solution. Divas such as *Acanthus mollis* need no support at all, nor do some of the larger ladies in the chorus such as *Phlox paniculata*, bless them. Penstemons and *Knautia macedonica* are like wild-eyed sopranos with big hair and will constantly escape from their supports and blowse charmingly all over the place for weeks whatever you do, so it is best not to bother. But a lot of the other big border players – the delphiniums we have already mentioned, and brittle things like *Galega officinalis*, *Salvia uliginosa* and *Cephalaria gigantea* – as well as countless others, are not worth growing unless you make an effort to support them, especially if your garden is windy. As I say, you get the hang of it all in due course.

Get them in early

Whatever method suits you and your plants, the key is to get your supports in early – definitely by mid-May – before the plants have grown too tall for you to get into the border without wreaking havoc. And tie them up loosely. Plants, like people, can't relax – and look utterly miserable – if their waistbands are too tight.

In the early days of your border, before you get to know who needs what by way of support, it might be as well to invest in a load of Y-stakes, curiously shaped bits of metal in various lengths, that are great for first-aid midsummer staking in new borders.

Deadheading

The reason that plants flower is to attract insects that pollinate them so that they can produce seeds, reproduce themselves and then, in the case of herbaceous plants, die back or die off completely. Once they have been pollinated and produced seeds, they stop flowering; the season's work is done. This is all very tedious for gardeners in summer, who want their plants to flower their socks off for as long as possible, while they deservedly sit back at last and enjoy the garden that has been their often exhausting obsession during the rest of the year. Deadheading is therefore the systematic removal of old, tired flowers almost before the plant realises what is happening, in order to fool it into producing new ones. That is all there is to it really, except that, depending on the type of plant, you can make it look even uglier if you fail to remove a section of stalk (down to where you can see the next flower bud emerging), as you remove the flower head. Plants that are forced to work so hard, in turn deserve extra feeding; a foliar feed with one of the 'steroids for

plants' variety, high in potash gives great rewards. If you are not familiar with foliar feeding, now is the time to become so. Plants can actually feed through their leaves, so all you do is mix up the recommended dilution of one of these wonder feeds, or you can use a seaweed-based organic one if you prefer, and swish over the entire border with a watering can, preferably in the early morning or in the evening. A great pick-me-up for all.

Deadheading is a labour of love, best carried out in the evening, kitchen scissors in one hand, a glass of wine in the other, and with a big old flower pot or one of those expensive Sussex trugs nearby in which to throw any bits you manage to catch. Or you can do it in the morning on your first pad round the garden *en pyjama*. It is one of the more satisfying and effortless border jobs and for me particularly so in the evening when a gentle meander provides a time when I can actually listen to my lovely blackbirds, to the sound of the water sploshing gently into my pond and breathe in all the wonderful gardeny, planty smells that are so powerful at the end of each day. It makes me forget all the mud and indecision, the backaches and writing deadlines and makes me realise why I still love gardening so much. Try it; you'll see.

The July chop aka the Hampton Court hack

By late July, even in the mildest and greyest of British summers, borders can start to run out of steam. Just as the grass slows down, so, in their way, do the borders. All the early flowerers, such as the pansies and geraniums have gone stringy. Deadheaded delphiniums and lupins are ragged and yellowing despite our best efforts. What the whole garden needs is a really good tidy-up and cut back. If you do this now, removing old foliage and stumpy old flower shoots by the barrow load, and if you can find the time and energy to then water, liquid feed, mulch and slug pellet everything at the same time, you can completely rejuvenate a border and kick-start it into late summer activity.

You need to be brave, and cut back much further than your instincts will allow. Cut pansies right back to the bone. Give the old tired shoots of geraniums a short, sharp tug and they will come completely away at the base, revealing the new foliage ready to put on a fresh performance. Take the shears to the catmint (give all the bits to your amazed and gratefully stoned cat), and cut all the old stems right out of the delphiniums. Of course, you will have to endure temporary gaps in the border here and there. But the whole process restores not only the garden's spirits, but also your own. It is thus a really worthwhile job to do. And if you are really organised and grown up about it, you will have some lilies or tobacco plants in big heavy pots waiting in the wings. Not to be planted, you understand, but to be stood with the blatant intent to deceive, in the 'holes' created by your late-in-the-day butchery in the border.

Watering

And so we come to watering, the bit people do generally less than efficiently. Presuming that you have chosen plants carefully, placed them in your border thoughtfully and done all the right things by them in the first instance, they should be able to get going in their first season without too much bother. Certainly a weekly check in the hottest part of the summer should suffice, to make sure that they are not suffering.

If and when you do have to water, water precisely, aiming the watering can or hose low down near the soil so that you reach the plants' roots and don't waste time and water soaking the leaves. Put a rose on the end of the watering can with a long spout, or use a hose with a rose end (I have an excellent lance-type hose end that reaches right into the back of the border). You should try to avoid anyone 'helpfully' applying violent jets of water to the soil/plants, which can make the border into a mud lake, and which in turn can damage the structure of the soil. And water *thoroughly*. A new plant needs to be encouraged to put its roots downward, eventually to find its own water. Too little a dose via a watering can or hose can be counterproductive, and only encourages surface rooting. In my new garden I have been quite tough and ruthless. I rarely water on the grounds that I am far too busy with other jobs to be a nursemaid to my plants. This hard-hearted attitude has led to generally good results, but it takes years to get out of the nurturing, molly-coddling frame of mind that seems to come all too naturally. As a rough rule of thumb, I would say that in a dry spell, a new, fast-growing shrub or perennial should have 10 litres (about 2 gallons) of water applied very slowly once a fortnight.

I am not a great fan of watering systems, but I have to admit that I've never had a 'pukka' one. I did resort to snaking a 'leaky hose' (the purpose-built porous pipe you can buy at garden centres) through the back of one of my London borders after a particularly arid summer but the next year it rained more, and I generally forgot to use it. The gardens I have seen that have proper watering systems all seem to change in character in a subtle way, not always for the better. Plants that previously coped without much water, luxuriating with frequently dampened feet, suddenly seemed to have a rush of blood to the head, put on a spurt of lush growth and start to dominate the garden, while at the back of the crowd, someone often gets missed out and languishes quietly. At the other end of the spectrum, I have seen expensively installed watering systems that have been completely mishandled. They are often turned on each day for too short a time, so that their equally expensive all-over layer of mulch is barely dampened, and the plants remain none the wiser as to the trouble to which their owners have gone to ensure their survival.

I suppose watering systems that are properly installed and managed can save busy gardeners a lot of time, but by turning on the garden tap you can be lulled into missing out on the daily garden inspection that is so pleasurable and vital. I find that watering, or deadheading, or checking on the plant supports are all essential parts of the relaxation buzz.

MIXED BORDER MEMORANDUM FOR THE YEAR

Summer

1 Check plant stakes and supports regularly. Delphiniums may need a 1.5m (5ft) cane per spire, tied in every 15cm (6in), not a ring of wire or string, otherwise they topple.

2 Deadhead all the time, removing stalks as well as heads, but let some biennials ripen seed before discarding them.

3 Cut back perennials that have done their best, to promote the

growth of new foliage and in some cases more flowers (I call this the Hampton Court Hack).

4 Thin out early-flowering shrubs, removing the shoots that have borne flowers and something larger from below, even if it means diving into the back of the border.

5 If unwanted gaps appear in the border, fill them with plants (lilies, perhaps, or even hastily bought tall annuals) in clay pots sunk into the soil, but do not forget to water them.

6 Treat mildew on roses, asters, phlox and so on, with a systemic fungicide.

7 Mulch and feed shrubs and roses in July, to give them a boost for the later summer.

8 Foliar feed the whole border, which will be 'tired' by July, using a high-potash feed to promote flowering.

Autumn

1 Continue deadheading until the battle is lost. In a wet season, more generous cutting back in July/August can provoke a surprisingly lush second flush of colour.

2 In late October, if you can hold off that long, *start* to cut down perennials' stems by half when they no longer look good, at a stroke removing a potential duvet of old stems and foliage for slugs, while leaving just enough top growth to remind you of their positions. Throw away spent annuals, and generally take stock of what needs to be done in the way of dividing, transplanting and replacing perennials.

3 Mulch established plants with compost or well-rotted manure. Always plant or replant with compost and plenty of organic stuff. Do not apply fertilisers high in nitrogen at this time of year.

4 Label plants, or leave markers or supports in situ – most herbaceous perennials completely die down in the winter.

5 Tidy up shrubs; there should be no need to prune heavily. Remove top weight from roses and spray them with systemic fungicide (see page 152) if they had shown signs of disease in late summer.

6 Plant daffodils and alliums as soon as you can, always in groups, and with a marker. Plant tulips in November.

7 Search the garden for self-sown seedlings – forget-me-nots, honesty, foxglove, etc. – and relocate them to fill up any gaps.

Winter

1 Remove any late-autumn growth from perennials; cut down to about 10cm (4in).

2 Put down slug pellets, or you could water the entire border with Slug Clear Liquid Concentrate which gets to the small black slugs that actually live in the soil and eat roots. Also keep the border free of drifts of dead leaves, which slugs and snails use as duvets.

3 Make sure that hardy fuchsias and any other tender perennials have a good dome of mulch over their bases – they will shoot earlier if protected from frost in this way.

4 Good lily bulbs become available in late winter. Do not buy them pre-packed. Go for fat, solid bulbs sold loose in boxes of peat or wood shavings. Plant them as soon as you get them if the ground is soft enough, (8cm) 3in down, with plenty of leafmould or compost, in groups of three or more. Put in markers or you will dig them up by mistake, or worse, put a spade through them.

Spring

1 Look out for pests early on – slugs remain active throughout a mild winter. Whitefly may appear on shrubs and climbers against warm walls (particularly honeysuckle) and aphids will attack early rose shoots. Use a systemic insecticide.

2 Prune roses and late-flowering shrubs. Apply a mulch around their bases and give them all a proper rose food (high in potash to encourage flower production).

3 Put plant stakes in place early, so that perennials can grow up through them.

4 Adjustments can be made in the border up to mid-April, but plant with even greater care and water well in hot weather.

5 If you did not apply much organic stuff to the rest of the border in the autumn do it now, together with a balanced fertiliser if you are so inclined. Take care not to damage emerging shoots. In late spring you can start foliar feeding with a soluble fertiliser, particularly if the weather is dry.

6 In late spring, plant out a few annuals. Do not be tempted to do this too early – there is no point – they will not get going until the soil warms up.

7 Cut back hardy fuchsias to the ground – even after a mild winter, when they will shoot out from quite high up on their previous growth. They make much better plants if cut down, but will start to flower a month or so later.

CHAPTER 6

Lawns – ghastly sparse grass

We shall not linger long on lawns

I often go on about the great gardening divide: chaps look after the lawn and guard every inch of it with their lives, likewise hedges, fences and other man-the-hunter, 'Englishman's home is his castle' stuff, while girls like flowers and all the pretty bits. Never mind about the passage of time having changed a lot of all that sort of stuff: if you think about the gardeners you know, I am sure you will agree that, whether you like the idea or not, broadly speaking this is true.

I do not know many women gardeners who are finicky about looking after the grass or boundary hedges, and I do not know many men who rule the roost in a mixed border (or, for that matter, many who actually bend in the middle enough to weed or grope around clearing old leaves from under shrubs... I could go on but I won't).

Of course you do get the odd neat-and-tidy women gardeners – the ones who put their (clean) wellies away all the time, wash their gardening gloves after every use and keep all their plant labels in a file in the kitchen drawer and off whose garden shed floors you could safely eat your dinner. These traitors to the cause will also doggedly slave away at the lawn edges before the arrival of guests, even sweeping up the bits, because they do not want tatty edges to ruin the look of their otherwise spotless, perfect gardens. But, on the whole, women are happy enough if the lawn is just green for most of the time, and appreciate the fact that grass is nicer to sit on and easier on their children's knees than any of the labour-saving alternatives. And the really soppy ones actually like daisies on the lawn because it reminds them of their schooldays.

A lawn, let it not be forgotten, is a closely packed collection of small herbaceous perennials that we walk on, jump up and down on, cut back

113

hard once a week for half of the year and abandon for the other half. It is no wonder, therefore, that small gardens in particular have bad lawns. Grass plants, just like other plants, need air, light, water and food to survive, and in the 'average family garden' (whatever that is), we seem to make life very difficult for them.

WHAT ARE THE MAIN CAUSES OF GHASTLY GRASS?

First, I will look in greater detail at what makes our lawns so dire and then, assuming (rather arrogantly) that you are true to your gender type and a bit of a lawn slacker, we will look at the minimum you can do to have a green lawn, and at which of the many boring lawn jobs are worth the effort.

Bad drainage

This is an awful, generally invisible problem that afflicts many new gardens, or gardens that have been 'landscaped', and is particularly common in areas of clay soil. Unsuspecting owners can be totally unaware that builders may have slapped down a load of turf as if they were carpet tiles (remember them? possibly not), over compacted subsoil on which JCBs and their like have been shunting around for weeks. The result is, come the winter rain, the garden can turn into a duck pond and, needless to say, grass doesn't like this much.

Overuse

There are generally areas of every lawn – entrances and exits from terraces, and around play areas, for example – that take such a battering that the soil beneath becomes too compacted for grass roots to survive. As a result, coarser, tougher and much less demanding plants – weeds and moss – start to take over. Even worse, the soil becomes alternately baked or waterlogged, so nothing at all will grow. The result is that you get completely bald patches that fail to green up in the spring, when even the worst lawns look their best.

Not enough light

Large shrubs and trees in small spaces form a dense canopy for the later part of the year, so grass becomes thin. Again, moss and weeds tolerant of shade and drought infiltrate the area (most troublesome is creeping buttercup, which marches across shady lawns at an alarming rate, throwing out runners in every direction). The grass is squeezed out and eventually packs up.

Bad mowing

Grass is either tended by a fanatic who, heavily influenced by cricket pitches, golf courses or rose-tinted memories of those immaculate green swards of childhood, mows it to a crisp, beige stubble every week. Or it suffers from haphazard occasional mowing by someone who doesn't give a fig, so once every so often the grass gets the shock of its life from which it takes ages to recover. Maybe, just maybe, I am exaggerating a bit, but I am sure you get the picture.

WHAT TO DO ABOUT THE ABOVE?

I should say at this point that it is not all the fault of rampant grassaholics. For many of us a garden is not a proper garden without grass. You should, however, consider the possibility of other surfaces if your garden is really, really small. Banish the words 'concrete' and 'jungle' from your mind – there are lots of ways of using paving, bricks and such like that will enhance a small garden in a way that an ailing patch of damp weedy grass will not. It can actually be a relief not to be constantly fussing over grass in a small hostile environment, and the garden can be usable for twelve months of the year and in most weather conditions. But if a lawn is what you absolutely have to have, then you should take on board the following and act on as much of the advice as you feel inclined to.

Do something about drainage

Drainage is an enormous problem in some gardens. Quite apart from the lawn, numerous plants will turn up their toes as a result of bad drainage. As far as grass is concerned, however, if the problem is localised and not too bad, you can, in the first instance, apply a sandy top dressing twice a year after removing plugs of turf with a hollow-tine aerator (more of that later). What you should not do is re-turf annually, without addressing the cause of the problem at all. I have known people do this, and one has to draw the conclusion that they must have more money than sense. For the same outlay they could have employed someone to put in a proper drainage system and solved the problem once and for all.

Walk this way

As for worn-out bits, think about strategically placed stepping stones on areas of unavoidable compaction. Set them very slightly below the level of the lawn so that you can mow straight over them without murdering the mower. Be aware that people and animals have a knack of making paths for themselves to get from A to B. They will do this rather than using those provided for them, subconsciously deciding that these take them from A to B via J or even W. By which I mean, have a look and see if your paths are in the right place, or whether by moving them, or doing a bit of transplanting or braver pruning, you would have a better-looking lawn – and a more cheerful lawn-keeper.

Playground solution

You could be really radical and give up trying to grow grass around children's play equipment; it makes mowing difficult anyway. Instead dedicate a small corner of the garden to all that dreadful plastic play stuff, keeping it on a bed of composted bark, edged with timber gravel boards. If you can't do this, you could adapt a neat trick I once saw: under a swing the owner of this garden had bedded a small piece of that rather nasty semi-rigid brown clematis support-mesh in the lawn. The presence of the mesh seemed to stop feet from scuffing the soil away, and helped the grass to survive. I expect ordinary dark green chicken wire would work just as well, and that you could also use the same method for protecting the grass at the end of a slide. You should, of course, make sure somehow that the corners are well anchored, so that they don't curl upwards and trip up small people.

Dealing with shade

If your grass starts off each spring looking reasonably chipper, but takes a bit of a nosedive in late summer, and if you have creeping buttercup invading your lawn, shade is very probably at the root of your problem. Take a critical look at your shrubs and any trees that hang over your garden. You can cut back the shrubs and often thin out the canopies of overhanging trees, or even remove a few lower branches. This will have a surprisingly dramatic effect, letting in more light and rain. Or you can have them pruned hard every two or three years. The proximity of trees to your precious lawn means that inevitably the ground will be deeply dry. An annual top dressing with a mixture that is heavy on peat or, preferably, something equally moisture-retentive will help the grass to survive.

Also, in shadier gardens, if the shrubs overhang the grass looking for light you should not be so mean with the size of your borders. Properly cut-out beds with shade-tolerant ground-cover plants, spring bulbs and so on, look far better than sparse grass petering out into barren soil. Be realistic, how much *usable* 'lawn' will you have lost? A smart move is to put in a mowing strip – a defining edge of brick or paving – and not let the grass or the border plants trespass into each other's territory.

While we are on the subject of defining edges, you can completely transform the look of a whole garden, whether it is shady or not, by giving your lawn an immaculately defined edge. It is not important whether you choose to go for broad sweeping curves (as opposed to indecisive nibbles in and out of encroaching shrubs), or for dead-straight formal edges. If those edges are cleanly cut, with a little gully at the edge of the border that collects wind-blown debris and makes maintenance easier, it will look as though someone knows what they are up to and has taken a bit of trouble, even if they don't and they haven't much.

Shade you can't manipulate – that which is cast by high walls or intransigent neighbour's trees, particularly conifers – can be a gardener's nightmare. The problem is compounded by extreme drought and acid soil that may be full of matted tree roots. This is another instance where it is not practical to keep on banging away at growing grass. You may just have to play around with the design of the garden so the no-go area can accommodate a shed, a climbing frame, a seating area or a beautiful pot, with or without something in it.

ROUTINE CHORES TO BENEFIT
EVEN THE WORST LAWNS

Mowing

Lawns under stress should not be mown too short. The turf of an ordinary garden is not the same as that of a golf course or bowling green. It consists of coarser and harder-wearing grasses and is meant to be kept longer. If mown too frequently or too short, it will weaken. Furthermore, domestic lawns are never really flat because of the use they get, so short mowing will result in the scalping of the high bits, which in turn will lead to the dying off of grass and the arrival of moss.

Start mowing, with the mower set on a high setting, as soon as the grass gets active – in towns that could be as early as late February. Between late April and mid-July it all gets rather hectic, with everything building to a once-a-week crescendo around the beginning of June. You can drop the height of the blade on the mower, but not to its lowest setting. With mowing, little and often is the key, and if you leave it for too long between cuts and have to mow it when it is several inches high – which means it is probably damp as well – it can look frightful afterwards.

Towards the end of the summer grass growth mercifully slows down so everything can be allowed to go a little beige. September rain causes a startling revival, and mowing at this end of the season, I find, is the most difficult to organise. In small, airless, sheltered gardens you may need to mow almost up to Christmas, but the grass is rarely dry enough. The only advice I can give is that you should seize the opportunities as they arise, and never put mowing off till another day.

A word about mowers: grassaholics, desperate for the day when they can play at being groundsmen and get a sit-on mower, may well yearn for a cylinder mower with a roller so that they can practise making stripes. These mowers do not cope with wet grass very well, clog up and cause a lot of bad language. Rotary mowers while not giving the same finish, cope with the long and/or wet grass far better. Their acquisition is therefore to be encouraged, if not insisted upon. Best still, though not in the least macho, are the latest lightweight lithium-ion battery mowers – a brilliant relief from boredom and drudgery. Again, take it from one who mows. More about mowers in the 'Batterie du jardin' chapter, page 194.

Raking

This is the job that hardly anyone does but it is one that makes a huge difference. At the end of the summer, rake out the build-up of dead grass and general mossy thatch using a special lawn rake. You can be quite tough. In fact, it is alarming what comes out, and at first you are convinced that you are pulling up all the grass. But only the weak or dead grass plants come out, along with Lego men's hats, sweet wrappers, ring pulls, small plastic farm animals, mystery apricot stones and countless brightly coloured bouncy balls. Amazing really. Do it again (but more gently because the grass is a bit fragile) in the spring, to 'raise the pile' as it were, before your first mow.

Aerating

Dedicated lawnists will derive a lot of satisfaction from this task, which is without doubt a really worthwhile, but mind-numbing, bit of hard graft.

If your overall drainage is bad, you will have to do a serious aeration job every other year in the spring or autumn, using a hollow-tine fork that actually removes little plugs of soil from the top 8cm (3in) of the lawn. You can hire these gizmos from hire shops, or share one with a similarly afflicted and dedicated neighbour, if you have one. It is really hard to get the fork into a compacted lawn and should not be attempted by the truly feeble, or when the lawn is anything other than soaking.

One year in my London garden (where the little lawn had to cope with upwards of 300 visitors tramping about on it one afternoon each year), I resorted to aerating the lawn in the middle of a downpour. It seemed to work a treat, and the water almost made plughole noises as it drained away to the outback down under. To make a really good job of it, you should then follow up with top dressing (see opposite), using a sandy mixture, which will help the drainage of the lawn considerably.

Those with less of a problem and still less enthusiasm, who perhaps want to improve the drainage in a small area of the lawn that has become compacted, can prod around with a garden fork. Even this is hard work, and I find the only way to do a decent job of getting the fork in deep enough is to throw it into the ground with all one's strength, then wiggle it around before pulling it out. Obviously the garden fork method does not do quite the same job as the hollow-tine fork, since you are not actually displacing any soil. But it is better than doing nothing at all.

Top dressing

This, particularly in conjunction with aerating described above, is *absolutely* the best thing you can do to a lawn, but should not be confused with fertilising. Top dressing involves adding a very thin layer of sandy-peaty soil to the lawn's surface. Some of it will find its way down the aeration holes, and will improve the drainage and condition of the lawn.

Top dressing, also sold as 'turf dressing', can be bought in bags from a garden centre although in my experience not all of them sell it. It is generally a 50/50 mixture of sand and peat or peat substitute. You could mix your own, but I think it is simpler to buy it ready bagged and add more sand or more moisture-retentive stuff depending on what your lawn problem is.

To spread it, you dump a large spadeful of the mixture at intervals of one square yard all over your lawn, and then brush it in with a stiff yard-broom. Do it when the grass is dry and freshly mown. When you have finished, you will hardly notice that you have done anything at all, so thin is the layer you have applied, so this is clearly not a job for those who need lots of appreciation for all their hard work. Grassaholics will want to go further and even out the bumps and dips with top dressing, but this is not really sensible and you are more likely to obliterate the grass in the dips than improve the situation to any noticeable degree. If grassaholics have got it that bad, they should acquire a proper lawn book and mug up on how to peel back the turf, add soil beneath it and then put it back. Well, quite!

Feeding

There is no law that says you have to feed your lawn, and many gardeners find the 'rush of blood to the head' green-ness lawns take on after they have been fed in the spring intensely unattractive. But if you care enough, and want your grass to go dark green and lush, then give it a high-nitrogen spring feed around the end of April, and again about five weeks later.

There are basically two kinds of feed: granular ones that may also contain weedkiller and moss control, and soluble ones you apply with a watering can or hose dispenser. Granular fertilisers are harder to apply, since you have to be precise or you can get pale 'stripes' where you miss bits out or burn marks where you overdo it. The best thing to do is buy, borrow or hire a little purpose-made trolley with holes in the bottom, and remember to overlap your wheel tracks. I used to use a granular feed for my rather weird-shaped little lawn, and it took some concentration to do it evenly; I had to take the phone off the hook and ignore both children and doorbell while I did it. I eventually worked out that the secret was to wheel the trolley very fast up and down the lawn, then repeat the performance, this time going across the garden so that it was hard to miss bits. I hated, absolutely hated, doing it, and in the end gave up and started to use soluble feeds. These are not as long lasting, and therefore have to be repeated every few weeks. But in my little garden it was far easier to swing a loaded watering can back and forth as I walked backwards down the lawn. The job was done in a matter of minutes.

So.much for the spring feed. The autumn feed, to my mind, is far more important and much less nerve-racking to apply. It is sold specifically as 'Autumn Lawn Feed' and is not interchangeable with the spring one, being low in nitrogen and high in phosphates to strengthen the grass roots for the winter. It does not produce that rush of blood to the head, nor is precision in applying it so important. In fact, if you are really clever, you can mix it in with your top dressing and spread it with a broom. You can also buy soluble autumn lawn food.

If you don't want to feed your lawn at all, then perhaps it is a good idea to leave your lawn clippings on the lawn after mowing just once during the summer. It will eventually break down into some sort of enriching feed, which is apparently better than doing nothing.

Watering

In an average year (what is that, we now ask ourselves?), British lawns go brown sometime in July, and go green again in late September. If water is in short supply – and we should all treat it as though it is – do not waste it on your lawn. You need an awful lot of water to do the job properly anyway, so look after your new shrubs and trees, but let the lawn do its own thing. The only exception, in my book, is new turf, which is an investment worth protecting, and needs regular watering until it becomes established.

Getting rid of weeds and moss

A healthy, regularly mowed lawn will, in theory, have far less of a weed and moss problem than a neglected and unloved one. And it is certainly true that most weeds peter out if they are mowed all the time. The exceptions are the nasty flat ones such as plantains, dandelions and creeping buttercup. Most of them can be dug out with a kitchen knife, and you can cramp the style of the buttercup by ripping out its runners. Or you could buy a spot weeder (a ready-mixed weedkiller spray or gel, such as Roundup) and apply a lethal dose to the centre of each offender.

I really hate using all-over weed- or moss-killer, so I don't. I know I am quite irrational about it, but I can't bear the idea of looking at all those sad patches once everything except the grass is dead. I do have patches of weeds here and there, but if I do nothing about them, what can I expect? And during the damper months at least lushness of the green sward in my present garden is definitely the result of having a positively disgraceful amount of soft green moss due largely to incessant East Sussex winter rain, slightly acid soil and an awful lot of shade. No, I belong quite unashamedly to the 'who cares as long as it's green' brigade.

Remedial work

Finally, whatever your basic attitude to your grass, just about every gardener needs to know how to do some or all of the following.

Reseeding bald patches

Using a hand-fork, loosen the top 5cm (2in) of soil, perhaps removing some and replacing it with fairly sandy potting compost such as John Innes No. 2. Mix some grass seed with a little of the compost and sprinkle it over the patch, firming it down with your hand or the back of a spade to make it level with the rest of the lawn. Water it very gently, using a very fine rose on the watering can. Cover the patch with a piece of chicken wire if you think it might get walked on in the first few weeks after germination (which will be just a matter of days between April to September). When the grass is about 5cm (2in) high, cut it once with shears. Thereafter you can mow it with the rest. It is important to realise that unless you have addressed the causes of the baldness you will probably have to over-seed (see opposite) at least once during the growing season.

Transplanting stray grass plants from borders

This is another highly effective (but slightly dotty-sounding) way of coping with small bald patches in the lawn. It is a modification of, shall we say, the Follically Challenged Footballer treatment (that's all I can get away with here). I am always weeding lawn-grass plants out of my borders. Instead of ditching them, I trim them and plant them in areas of thin grass or in small bald patches. They actually 'take' very quickly because they already have good roots, and the patch becomes undetectable within a week or so. This is something I used to do a lot and with excellent results in my old small garden, thought it was a bit silly when I had acres of grass to tend, but have started doing it again in my newer (smaller) one.

Over-seeding a tired lawn

In early autumn, once the mowing has slackened off, or in spring before it has gone into top gear, you can over-seed a thin lawn: that is, add fresh seed to the existing lawn without much preparation. I generally add grass seed to top dressing and do it this way. It does help to thicken things up.

Turf patching

This is a skill I had to acquire to deal with a rough old country lawn. I mention it here because I am amazed how unskilled you need to be to patch your own grass using turf from another part of the same lawn. The point about it is that the grasses automatically 'match', as does the level of soil fertility. It becomes a case of invisible mending within weeks – far better than patching with posh imported turf or re-seeding, which will both take years to blend in. So if you need to re-turf an area, see if you can steal from another part of the lawn. (And go on; make that border bigger while you are at it.)

CHAPTER 7

Disentangling roses

There seems to be something particularly irresistible about roses – still, in the twenty-first century, the nation's favourite flower. But growing roses well and getting the most out of them in a small space needs considerable effort since, despite their allure, roses are troublesome. Putting it baldly, they are ugly, prickly, disease-prone bushes, most of which do not fit in with the accepted gardening wisdom that shrubs should have more than one thing going for them in order to earn their keep. Even minimal rose maintenance takes up an extraordinary amount of precious gardening time, time we would far rather spend deadheading the dahlias, training the trachelospermum or even getting seriously stuck into the renovation of a tired old winter jasmine.

Despite their shortcomings as garden plants, we are apparently bewitched. How many of us I wonder, have at some point fallen for a rose – for its scent maybe, for its subtle colouring or maybe even for its daft name – for which we realistically have no space? And have we then shoved it in a container (they don't like containers) and watched it gradually become so manky that it eventually has to be chucked away or hidden somewhere with all the other dead things 'round the side' or 'at the back' (we all have graveyards).

And then there are those gardeners who develop a grand and all-consuming passion for roses, even giving over most of their gardens to growing a tangle of old shrub roses that only flower for about two or three weeks of the year: the 'pray it doesn't rain, don't blink or you'll miss them' kind of plants, like those other traitors, paeonies (which the same deluded gardeners probably also grow). These poor souls relish rolling off the tongue the impossible French names of their favourites – 'Madame de Zees', 'Souvenir de Zatte' and 'Comtessse de Zee Ozere' –

127

to anyone who will listen. (It may help to remember that these gardeners can't all be experts, and can probably only remember and pronounce the names of the roses they themselves grow.)

Even those who are not particularly enamoured of them probably have a rose bush tucked away in their garden somewhere, probably one that, for illogical and vaguely sentimental reasons they have so far failed to ditch but which could, with a bit of knowledge and effort, be restored to vigour and beauty. And while it doesn't matter two hoots what that rose is called, it does matter what kind of rose it is – be it a Hybrid Tea, a Floribunda, a shrub rose of some kind, or a climber or rambler. Because unless you know at least this much about your roses, you don't know what to expect from them or how to look after them. The first thing I will do, therefore, is give simple basic descriptions of the various rose types. I don't think it is particularly necessary to name lots of names: 'what is what' is more helpful than 'who is who' when it is all a bit of a fog.

Bush roses

This is the name often applied to Hybrid Tea roses and Floribunda (or 'multicluster') roses bred in the early part of the last century, after the creation of the National Rose Society and an upsurge of interest in rose breeding. They are sold by the thousands every year and are the most popular of roses.

Hybrid Tea roses

These are tall, slim bushes bearing elegant blooms on long stems over a long period during the summer. The flowers are double, often heavily scented and beautifully formed, and are carried singly or with smaller side buds. They are the ideal roses for cutting to put in vases (to go on

128

a beautiful mahogany table, the sunlight from an open casement window filtering through their perfect petals ...). The bushes themselves are quite difficult to accommodate comfortably in a mixed border or a stuffed, shrubby town garden, because of their innate gauntness, and the way in which you have to prune them down each year. Both they and the Floribundas (below) look much better grown en masse in the sort of rose beds our grandfathers favoured; they can be seen this way, should you wish to do so, in places such as Regent's Park. Generally it is these bedding roses people inherit from previous owners and that need to be 'renovated' or removed because they have become so diseased and ugly through ignorance and/or neglect.

Floribunda or multicluster roses

These are usually, but not always, smaller, wider-spreading bushes that have much more of a rag-bag look to them, with larger clusters of often quite garish flowers that are not generally strongly scented. There are usually two major flushes of flowers in mid- and late summer. Some of these roses are quite useful, adding colour and substance to a mixed border but, again, their natural home is a proper rose bed.

Shrub roses

Shrub roses are quite different in character from bush roses. As the name suggests, these are the roses for a relaxed shrub garden or mixed border, and some are useful for making flowering hedges. There are many different types within this group. The whole issue is immensely complicated, but the feature these roses generally have in common is their softness of outline.

A BRIEF RUNDOWN OF SOME SHRUB ROSES YOU MAY ENCOUNTER

Species roses – wild roses and near relations
Modern Shrub roses – twentieth-century-bred roses with some Floribunda characteristics, often repeat flowering and lightly scented

Old Shrub roses – bred in the nineteenth century; a lot of them have French names and most of them only flower once

Hybrid Perpetuals and Hybrid Musks – hybrids of old roses, as the name suggests, bred for their ability to repeat flower

English roses – twentieth-century roses with some characteristics of old shrub roses

Rugosa roses – a slight oddity from Japan, with crinkly leaves, scented flowers and large colourful hips

Suggested uses

Some shrub roses flower only once but spectacularly, often leaving enormous and decorative hips as a reminder of their splendour. Indeed, roses such as *Rosa glauca* are grown chiefly for their orange hips (in this case contrasting well with its thunder-cloud-coloured foliage).

Many of the bigger shrub roses need a surprising amount of space and only really come into their own if they are allowed it without let or hindrance. Others, such as the popular modern shrubs, 'Ballerina', 'Fairy' and 'Magic Carpet' have a very long flowering period and being small and neat of bloom can fit into the tiniest of gardens. And, of course, there are those rather (in my view) wretched, tiny things called Patio roses.

The best, most useful roses combine a long flowering period, good scent, strong arching growth and a good overall shape. Many of my own favourites are the English roses such as 'Gertrude Jekyll' and 'Sweet Juliet', and Hybrid Musks ('Penelope', 'Buff Beauty', 'Prosperity', 'Felicia', 'Moonlight' and others – note the generally sensible English names), some of them giving off that heady old-ladies-hand-cream scent. But then, everyone who grows roses (by design rather than by accident) has favourites.

Climbing and rambling roses

These are used for climbing and screening purposes. This may sound like stating the obvious, but climbers climb, and ramblers ramble. A lot of gardeners think the names are interchangeable but they aren't. There are important differences when it comes to their type of growth, management and maintenance for reasons which I hope will become clear.

Climbing roses

The growth of true climbing roses forms a woody framework consisting of a few rather stiff stems. The framework changes little once the plant is mature. Many of them have been bred from Hybrid Tea roses, and like them, carry single, scented blooms over a very long period. There are two basic types, vigorous – which are often mistakenly referred to as 'ramblers' – and non-vigorous, some of which look like rather stretched Hybrid Teas and don't climb very far at all. If you wanted to choose a rose to go up a wall or over an arch to occupy a clearly defined space you should pick one that says 'climber' on the label rather than 'rambler' – or even go for one of the lanker shrub roses (see opposite) such as 'Penelope'.

To approach things from the other way, if you have a rose climbing up your house with an enormous rather bare woody base with not much new growth on it, while somewhere under the first floor windows it produces a succession of flowers throughout the summer that you can hardly see, let alone smell, pick or deadhead, this is most probably a maltreated climber.

Rambling roses

Unlike climbers, rambling roses are generally recognised by their extremely vigorous growth, with several long pliable stems being produced from close to the base of the plant each season. Many of them carry huge and spectacular trusses of, in some cases, rather small flowers over a period of about three weeks in midsummer. Following this they put out a fresh crop of long shoots that by October drive any neat and tidy gardeners mad, with often disastrous results for both rose and pruner. Many ramblers are prone to mildew, especially if they are grown on house walls or in other restricted, airless spaces. Another problem with them is that they really need tricky midsummer pruning unless grown up trees, which is where they look and perform best. Frankly, if you have a rambler in a place where there is not enough space to allow it to do its own thing, it can be a pain to live with. For midsummer drama, however, ramblers are unsurpassed.

PRUNING ROSES

As you might expect, different types of rose require different treatment where pruning is concerned. If you have understood and grasped the basic guidelines for pruning shrubs, it will help considerably in the understanding of rose pruning if you forget all the mystique surrounding the subject and look at roses just as you would other shrubs. Think of them as late or early flowerers (i.e. those that flower on the current or the previous season's growth), and therefore need to be 'renovated' at appropriate times of the year, and encouraged to produce new shoots on which to flower.

Pruning late-flowering roses

Hybrid Tea and Floribunda roses (which are both bush roses), plus Modern Shrub roses fall into the 'late' category, flowering on wood produced in the current year – in the same way as, say, a *Buddleja davidii* or a lavender does. They, therefore, should be pruned at some time in the winter or very early spring, when they are dormant, so that they can produce new shoots during the late spring that will flower from midsummer onwards.

How much to prune bush roses (the most commonly grown roses) has always been the subject of much discussion among gardeners. My parents' generation – with their traditional rose beds – were happy to hard-prune their Hybrid Teas and Floribundas, cutting them back almost to the ground each year in about February. The results were late- but larger-flowering roses, healthy because they had all the nasty bits automatically cut out of them – and for those reasons they were happy to put up with looking at a barren garden-scape for several months of the year.

More recently it has become accepted practice to prune bush roses and most modern shrubs less hard – to about half their full height, but to be ruthless about cutting out weaker or damaged growth from close to the base of each rose. This is known as 'medium pruning', and should be carried out between January and March.

The key to the whole procedure is to work strictly from the base of the bush. By all means have a tweak about and remove some of the heavy hips and a few inches of top growth before the winter winds buffet everything about, to prevent the roots from loosening. This is not proper pruning, however, and later in the season you have to be much braver than your instincts tell you. The harder you prune a rose, the more it will grow – if a rose is unhealthy, prune it more, not less.

Step-by-step guide to medium pruning

1 Crouch or sit on the ground so you are working on the base of the bush. Ignore everything above your head. Don't look up or you might chicken out of what you are about to do.

2 Using sharp secateurs – not the ones you have ruined by cutting garden wire, letting them rust in the rain, etc. – cut out all dead (brown, brittle) and diseased or injured wood from its source and remove from ground level the thickest and brownest stems, which are the oldest and therefore the least productive. On a neglected rose, this may be most of what is there, and you may need a small-bladed pruning saw to get through the branches because they are so thick. Don't waver, just do it.

3 Next, cut out all very skinny stems and ones that grow across the bush or touch others.

4 Cut out any immature wood (bendy and with soft thorns) that has grown late in the season from near the base of the bush.

5 Only thick, green and healthy stems should now remain. Cut

these down to an outward facing 'eye' or leaf scar – with careful scrutiny you can find one of these on even quite old stems. It is from *these* scars that the new shoots will come. The cut should be slanting, with the 'eye' about a centimetre below the high point of the slant. The aim is to create a framework of perhaps three or four (in the case of Hybrid Teas) or half a dozen (in the case of Floribundas and shrubs) vigorous shoots that will form an almost candelabra-shaped bush once they shoot out. The final height of the pruned rose should be about half that of the un-pruned bush you started with, which will be somewhere between 30cm (1ft) and 75cm (2½ft).

6 Pick up the bits, remove any weeds from around the base of the bush, loosen the top few centimetres of soil carefully with a hand fork, apply rose food and mulch. The truly dedicated will spray the rose with a systemic fungicide, which can be absorbed through the stems to prevent mildew, rust and black spot from developing later in the season.

Radical cuts

Experiments have been carried out in the past few years simply pruning roses with hedge trimmers. Early results were amazing, with the bushes flowering profusely. Given the way roses grow, dying back within themselves, congested stems injuring each other with their thorns and becoming prey to disease, I would guess that after a while this method of pruning will fall out of favour, as I can't imagine that, in the long run, it will produce anything other than ugly, gradually weakening and diseased bushes. Time will tell.

Pruning climbers

It is very difficult to lay down hard-and-fast rules about pruning any types of rose – particularly climbers and ramblers, because how you do it depends so much on what you want the roses to do for you, how far you want them to climb, how much of their growth you can reach and how bothered you are about their performance. I think it is important, however little you do, that you understand what the plant will do as a result of your action (or inaction).

Climbers flower on current season's shoots and should, like bush roses, also be pruned in the winter or early spring. The short shoots that have borne flowers should be cut back to within a few buds or 'eyes' – leaf scars – of the main woody framework of the plant. To put it another way, this is a relatively simple operation involving cutting back all the shoots that have got hips on them to short stumps about 10cm (4in) long. In the winter if you go and look at a climber that has been pruned by a professionally trained gardener for years, you will notice an immaculately trained framework of branches, probably attached by neatly tied twine to stout horizontal wires if it is on a wall, with short stumps sticking out off the framework all along its length. This is a far cry from the messes most of us live with, and it is both humbling and educational.

A well-fed, happy climber will generally produce a good stout shoot from near the base every other year or so. Unfortunately, this thick, straight green shoot often looks so at odds with the remainder of the brown, gnarled rose that compulsive pruners frequently shriek 'sucker!' and with a manic gleam in their eyes, cut it (or them) clean off.

What you should actually do is thank your lucky stars the rose has produced such a wonderful thing. As you do so, bend it gently into a position that follows the rest of the framework and tie it in loosely before the end of the summer, before it becomes rigid and brittle (at which point it might snap if you try to bend it). Come the winter you can then remove one of the old shoots of the framework with secateurs. This way a climber gradually renews itself and doesn't become an ugly monster, yawning menacingly away from its support and eventually breaking away completely.

Dealing with monsters

If you already have an ugly monster of a climber, feed and mulch it for a year and remove the worst and knobbiest shoot from as close to the bottom of the framework as you can. The rose will thus be forced into action once again and you can start to train subsequent new shoots into position and go on from there. Banish axe-men pruners from that area of the garden for fear of grave misdemeanours.

In the worst cases – where you have to remove a rose from a house wall or archway in order to carry out building repairs for example – you can, for once, call on the services of that itchy-fingered axe man and cut the whole rose down to the ground to make it start again. You will get no flowers for a year or two while it does, however. This drastic action applies to all kinds of overgrown roses, not just climbers. Old, well-established roses are the most robust of plants and remarkably hard to kill; it is quite difficult to see what all the fuss is about.

Pruning early-flowering roses

Next we should look at ramblers and Old Shrub roses that flower once on the previous season's growth. Relating these to the shrub-pruning guidelines, they fall roughly into the 'early-flowering' weigela or philadelphus category. They therefore need to have their tired flower shoots removed and should be tidied up in mid-season immediately after flowering, to encourage them to produce plenty of new shoots for the following year. Of these two groups, ramblers are the trickiest, and the vigorous small-flowered varieties the very worst.

Ramblers

Since they flower mostly on wood produced at the back end of the previous year, ramblers should be pruned immediately after flowering unless of course they are growing out of reach up trees or other large structures. It is a devoted soul indeed who gets really stuck in during the hottest part of the year and prunes out the oldest huge shoots of a prickly rambler from ground level and deadheads the rest, in order to make way for the following year's flowering shoots produced during the surge of new growth that is about to happen. In our London garden, we shared a stunning 'Rambling Rector' (the ultimate extrovert, despite his name) with our lovely neighbours. Pruning him became an annual social event. Everyone used to stand around watching and drinking tea while I teetered up a ladder suffering appalling lacerations. On reflection, it seems that most real gardeners have scratched arms in summer.

I have to say that I now bend the rules a bit. I have a half-hearted go during late summer at cutting off any old flowers I can reach as well as thinning out and removing some of the new shoots that appear higher up and make the rose look bothersomely tangled. But I often wait until the rose has lost its leaves in winter, when I can see what I am doing a little better, before cutting out more old wood. I still reserve plenty of long new shoots and tie them in place, which is easy to do since, unlike the shoots of a climber, they remain pliable. There is generally so much new growth produced that I can easily afford to cut out and sacrifice some of it, slim the whole rose down and make a much better fist of the whole job.

What you should definitely not do is 'tidy up' a rambler in the autumn and winter by cutting back all the new shoots that are waving in the breeze. If you do, the following year's flowering will be very much reduced. If you do it every year, the rose will for ever have a look of an ugly hedgehog about it.

Old Shrub roses
These behave similarly to ramblers in that they are 'early' flowerers, producing blooms on growth made the previous year, and should have old shoots removed after flowering or during the winter when you can get at them better. The newer shoots should be tinkered with as little as possible.

More general rosey-pruning stuff

If you become seriously addicted to shrub roses (and many of us do, be they 'Old' or 'Modern'), it is worth finding out more about the pruning of each specific group. Here are a few pointers:

 1 Hybrid Perpetuals appreciate having their newer stems arched over and pegged down.
 2 In addition to a spring prune, my beloved Hybrid Musks need an additional really good midsummer cut back (by 30cm/12in or more) to encourage a prolific autumn flush of flowers.

3 English Roses (modern shrubs that flower in the current season, remember) despite their lax 'old rose' habit, benefit from quite surprisingly hard spring pruning to create new growth sufficiently robust to support their heavy flowers.

4 Small prolific roses such as 'The Fairy', should be pruned in the early spring more as you would Floribundas, opening out the middle of the bush, removing much of the congested skinny growth, cutting the rest down by about half in early spring.

5 If shrub roses have good autumn hips, only remove half of the old flowers. You can go back in the winter and smarten them up by removing any old wrinkled relics that the birds have left behind. Hip-bearing Rosa glauca, however, flowers on new shoots, and spring pruning produces shoots and leaves that are superbly coloured.

6 As a general rule, never cut off any strong new growth that comes from the base of any rose.

Experiment and do some research

Having written all of the above, I do appreciate that learning to prune anything from verbal instructions – or even worse, from illustrations in a book – is extremely hard. You go out there armed to the teeth with posh new secateurs, a little shiny saw, your smartest pruning gloves and a brain full of instructions, only to find that somehow your own roses bear absolutely no relation to the ones described and illustrated in your books. Before you know it, your resolve has weakened and you find yourself twiddling around removing a few old rose hips and then going off to have a cup of coffee and count the fish in the pond again or talk to the robin.

If you are completely foxed, you could try to get someone who knows the ropes to show you how to do it. The Royal Horticultural Society and some horticulture colleges run pruning demonstrations, which many years ago I found helpful. But if you really feel confused and care about getting it right, and there is no one to help, take heart. Rome wasn't built in a day. Most of us taught ourselves by trial and error, and roses are very tolerant. Make a note or take pictures of your roses after you have pruned them. If they look ugly or don't flower well one year, do something different the next and you'll get there in the end.

It can be awe-inspiring and very helpful to visit a proper rose garden – Mottisfont Abbey in Hampshire and Sissinghurst Castle in Kent for example – and see how many ways there are to train and prune roses. If you go in the winter when the leaves have dropped, you can get a good look at how the training is done, and maybe even find a friendly gardener whose brains you can gently pick. Take a notebook and a camera. There is a lot to be learnt about roses.

BUYING, PLANTING AND FEEDING ROSES

There was a time, not so very long ago, when roses were only sold bare-rooted in the winter, and you could not get hold of them at all during the growing season. In fact, this is probably the best way to buy roses. Planted while dormant, they can settle into their new soil and grow away without a hiccup in the following spring.

Plant roses much in the same way as you would other shrubs, with plenty of organic matter and bonemeal or a special rose fertiliser or mycorrhizal fungi (see page 22). Tidy up any damaged roots using secateurs and make sure you do not end up with an air pocket underneath the plant (fiddle the soil in between the roots carefully with your fingers). Most roses are propagated by being grafted on to wild rootstock, the graft forming a knobbly bit between the roots and stem of the plant. This is a potentially vulnerable part of the rose and after planting should be at or just below soil level, barely visible. If it ends up sticking up out of the soil, start your planting process again; likewise if you end up with the green stems below soil level. You should avoid being a lazy daisy, trying to build up the soil level around the graft or

139

excavating a small ditch around it and hoping for the best. Take it from me, it does not work.

These days, roses are more often presented to us in 2-litre pots at any time of the year, and are often sold in full flower. Planting them in the ground at this time is a touch and go operation, since roses do not make a fine network of roots to create a root ball as most other woody plants do. I should stress that it is far easier and safer to plant roses when they are dormant and leafless (if you can bear to hold off until the late autumn), when they will be as tough as if they were bare-rooted. You can, however, with a bit of care, get away with doing it all wrong... I have actually used the following technique with great success.

Planting a rose while in full flower
(if you absolutely have to...)

1 Prepare the ground deeply in the usual way (adding organic stuff, bonemeal or rose fertiliser).
2 Water the potted rose well.
3 Snuggle the rose (still in its pot) down into the soft prepared soil until its graft is at the correct level in relation to the soil around it.
4 Press the soil around the pot to compact it slightly, then water it deeply and wait a few minutes for the ground to sop up most of the wet.
5 Gently pull the pot and rose out of the ground, leaving a perfect imprint behind in the soil.
6 With bated breath and one swift and confident movement, invert the pot while holding the rose graft between your fingers, remove the pot and deftly slot the rose into position.
7 Apply a mulch and tiptoe away – the rose may not even notice its change of circumstances.

NB: If planting a new rose in the place of an old one, you should completely replace a substantial amount of soil (a patch at least 40cm/16in deep and wide) with soil taken from somewhere else in the garden (the old soil is harmless elsewhere and can perhaps be used as 'top dressing' for tired patches of lawn). You can also use mycorrhizal fungi (see page 22) as you plant the newcomer, making sure that it comes in contact with its bare roots.

Pruning newly planted roses

The usual advice that you should prune down a newly planted rose is very hard to follow, but is generally worth taking. If a rose has been grown in a container, the growth can often be twisted and spindly. By pruning it right down in the first spring after planting, you can kick-start its growth anew. This is particularly important with climbing roses, which need a good stout framework from the start. I have been far too impatient in the past to see a rose do something pretty in its first season, and have often regretted not being more strong-minded.

Mind you, there was that memorable occasion when I did do everything right, and had to wait for the best part of eighteen months to see a rose flower for the first time, only to find that it had been mis-labelled. Much cursing ensued, but as is so often the way with plants and gardens, if not in other parts of one's life, the gate-crasher proved to be the life and soul of the party. I never actually bothered to find out who the interloper was – it was a scented shrub rose that flowered twice each year – but it was absolutely wonderful.

The fuss about suckers

Subsequent damage to a grafted rose below soil level can result in the production of suckers. On standard roses (put basically, rose bushes that have tall 'trunks'), suckers can shoot out of the 'trunks', since the graft knobble is at the top, just below the point where the rose branches are produced. Suckers are identifiable by looking at the overall colour of the shoot, and not necessarily, as is popularly believed, by counting the number of leaflets. Suckers are generally a pale, matt colour, quite different from the darker, shinier leaves of the proper rose. They should always be removed, because growing, as they do, from a vigorous wild rose root they can sap away the strength of the grafted rose and overwhelm it.

If you prune off a sucker, even below soil level, it will shoot from lower dormant buds and you will probably get two more as a reward for your efforts. The answer is to trace them back to the root from which the sucker or suckers have grown and wrench them off, destroying as you do so the possibility of the sucker growing from another dormant bud. (In fact, the chances are that, if you have a wild rose growing in your garden, it is a sucker that has taken over from a maltreated and neglected cultivated rose.)

Feeding

Roses appreciate a feed twice a year, in March and July, with a proper rose fertiliser. Rose food is higher in potash than general garden fertilisers, and potash, remember, makes roses and other flowering plants do really well; it also contains various trace elements that they appreciate. Roses benefit particularly from having their root area covered with well-rotted horse manure in spring. I have also used a soluble rose feed which seemed excellent, but had to be applied once a week during the entire growing season, thereby providing the overstretched gardener with something else to remember to do. I instinctively feel, however, that the soluble feed hits the spot better during the dry weather of high summer, after the roses have had their first flush of flower. The recommended July granular feed needs to be rained on or otherwise watered in, or it can just sit on the surface and do nothing.

Pests and problems

In Chapter 8, dealing with plant pests and diseases, I have outlined most of the troubles that afflict roses and mentioned solutions and remedies. The most common pests are aphids and leafhoppers, and the most difficult diseases to control are mildew, black spot and rust.

I regret to say that I have personally never seen perfect roses grown without the use of chemical sprays, and the fact that I grow roses (and those rust-magnets, hollyhocks) is the main reason I draw back from being a totally organic gardener. The all-in-one systemic insecticide/ fungicide cocktail rose sprays simplify the whole pest/disease control issue, but the new, 'greener' me prefers to only use a systemic insecticide if absolutely necessary early in the season, and a systemic fungicide as a preventative measure (for plants that are known to have been diseased the previous season, for example), or at the first signs of trouble – usually around July.

Roses occasionally suffer from iron-deficiency chlorosis which can be sorted out with a dose of Sequestrene, and sometimes suffer from physiological disorders – mineral deficiency, for example – that can generally be remedied by starting to use a proper rose fertiliser.

I hate to be harsh about plants that have such a special place in our affections, but in my view it all comes down to the inescapable fact that if you love roses, alas, you have to work at them. And if you haven't got time, or the attitude to work at them, you shouldn't grow them.

And finally...

Most roses need sun, hate draughty corners, like growing in heavy-ish soil that is never waterlogged, and seem to be happiest in soil with a neutral pH, although they will cope with acid or limey soil. Roses, once established, develop into extremely tough, strong-rooted plants that can live and flourish for thirty years or more. They are quite vulnerable for the first year or so and should be checked every spring to make sure that they have not loosened in the soil – they should be trodden well in again if they have.

CHAPTER 8

The undesirables – pests, diseases and weeds

Iwill come clean straight away – in case you haven't twigged: organic gardener I am not. Those who are will tell you with evangelistic zeal that until you bite the bullet and go the whole hog (don't you love the juxtaposition of those two?), you will be cast into utter darkness in the hereafter, but that's as may be.

It is all too easy, especially in small, hemmed-in gardens without a big enough population of natural predators, for your shrubs to shrivel, your roses to go ropey and for your borders to be bitten to bits. As even the most ardent organic gardener will tell you, if they are being really truthful, dealing with pests and diseases organically can be a bit of a hit and miss affair and quite a lot of work. I am as 'green' as I can be in other ways, composting, recycling, mulching to save water, using organic fertilisers – but I still find it necessary to kill some pests and treat some diseases with the few garden chemicals still available to us. I know this attitude is bound to alarm and infuriate the 'all or nothing' brigade and I realise that to an extent I am – as are those many gardeners whom I know share my attitude – on borrowed time, as one by one the effective chemicals available to amateur gardeners vanish from the shelves. At time of writing, research is showing that the chemicals currently in the systemic insecticides used by gardeners (and to a far greater extent by farmers, of course) may well be responsible in part for the devastation of our bee population. The jury is, as they say, 'out'. But for how much longer?

PESTS

Even though I have confessed to dragging my heels on the whole issue, I have to admit there are some garden pests that can be adequately controlled by natural means, and this is the way forward for gardeners who really don't want to use the few insecticides that are still available to us. Biological control is a term that is applied to the exploitation of the 'dog-eat-dog' aspect of the battle against pests, and involves introducing natural predators of a given baddie into a controllable environment and letting them do their worst. Apart from the slug and vine-weevil soil-drenches containing appropriately predatory nematodes (with which you may already be familiar), many of the controls available involve flying or crawling parasites, and so are only really practical for use in greenhouses and conservatories. If you need to find out more, the Royal Horticultural Society website (see page 201) has all the latest information on this kind of pest control.

Here follows a brief rundown of the most common garden leaf nibblers, munchers and general plant-wreckers. It isn't intended to be comprehensive since there are loads of illustrated books by real experts on the subject, and you can of course find pictures and information on the internet. If you cannot identify a problem, someone at your local garden centre or nursery may be able to help (take freshly collected specimens in clear, sealed plastic bags).

Slugs and snails are consistently top of the list of most hated nasties. They are chiefly active at night during damp weather and in bad summers are almost uncontrollable. You can, of course, do your best to seek and destroy – go out at night with a torch and a bucket of salty water into which to plop your victims. It has been proved, incidentally, that if you fling snails over the fence, they will come back the next day, so don't. You can be equally evil by enticing slugs and snails out during dry spells by 'watering' foliage with a water-soluble version of a slug/snail killer (such as Slug Clear). Yesss.

In dry weather at any time of year huge gangs of snails can be found holed up in ivy-covered walls (unlike slugs, snails can climb and are

146

often to be found bivouacking up trees) and almost interleaved in stacks of empty plant pots. Slugs, meanwhile, will go to ground under stones or worm their way into your compost bin. In fact the big fatties do the least damage – it is the small, black, soil-dwelling slugs that do most of the root-and-shoot munching, while the beige ones that lurk in lawns can destroy daffodil flowers overnight.

There are slug/snail pellets suitable for organic and inorganic gardeners, of course. Or you can wait until the soil warms up in spring and use a biological control that you water into the ground (it involves nematodes that burrow into the slugs and eat them from within). It is all-out war, really: you can put down beer traps and build barriers of materials over which they can't/won't ooze (gritty substances, mostly) around special plants and pots. Slugs and snails get mild electric shocks if they try to slither over copper, and there is a sticky copper tape on the market that, if used imaginatively around pots, is extremely helpful.

At the time of writing, my barrier of choice is an ingenious product made out of the nasty bits at the back ends of sheep – a mixture of wool and sheep poo in pellet form. Used as a mulch around mollusc-beloved plants it keeps them at bay while feeding the plants as well.

Aphids are known as 'greenfly' or 'blackfly' to most of us, although some of them don't actually have wings at all. After a mild winter, aphids can get going surprisingly early, so be on guard from February onwards. They can be severely damaging in gardens where there is only a small bird population to keep them in check, especially to early-flowering honeysuckles, where attacks by blackfly can go unseen actually within the shoot tips. They are nearly always found in writhing clusters on rose shoots, chiefly in the first half of the summer.

Aphids also attack the new shoots of shrubs that are produced after mid-season pruning – for example, the new growth of philadelphus and some viburnums can be virtually destroyed by clusters of blackfly that hide in their shoot tips in July and August. To control aphids, spray plants with a systemic insecticide (those that are absorbed through the plant's leaves, see page 156).

Years ago, a gardening student of mine who shunned the use of chemicals in her garden used to swear blind she had no greenfly in her London garden. I discovered the secret of her success: she used to remove her specs when she went out into the garden. Well, I suppose it is one way of (not) looking at things.

Whitefly are actually tiny white moth-y creatures that live on the underside of leaves. They are mainly a greenhouse or conservatory pest (for which there is a biological control in the form of a parasitic wasp), but they do enjoy enclosed and sheltered areas in mild gardens, where they proliferate – particularly on climbers and wall shrubs. As soon as you see trouble, you should spray with a systemic insecticide. You will probably have to repeat the process at fairly frequent intervals. For potted plants indoors where spraying is inadvisable, I use (rather expensive) impregnated little insecticidal sticks that you shove into the compost – preferably before a bad infestation takes hold.

Leafhoppers also live on the underside of leaves, and are often confused with whitefly. If you look closely, however, they look more like tiny greenish grasshoppers with big wings. When disturbed, they have a less dizzy-moth-y flight pattern than whitefly. In sheltered gardens they seem to do most damage on roses, tobacco plants and sages. Leafhoppers disfigure leaves by sucking sap and making them appear slightly bleached. There is a super-huge leafhopper that hangs out around rhododendrons in midsummer and can spread the fungal spores that cause bud blast (black, slightly bristly flower buds that fail to open) on rhododendrons. It is definitely worth having a go at this one with a systemic insecticide and, at the same time, you should try to remove any old blackened buds that are still attached to the bushes.

Froghoppers make 'cuckoo-spit' when they are tiny in spring, most noticeably on lavender and rosemary. The 'spit' eventually disappears, by which time the ugly little nymphs inside it have become even uglier brown, hopping frog-like bugs that suck sap and do a lot of damage. If you can bear it, pick them off by hand and squash them when they are still in the 'spit', which unfortunately acts as an effective shield against any chemicals and natural predators.

Caterpillars eventually become beautiful butterflies and moths, and unless your garden is being seriously eaten up, show a little mercy. If the problem is intolerable, it really is best to steel yourself and pick them off by hand – they generally attack one plant at a time. You could try squashing the eggs that butterflies lay on the backs of leaves, if you catch them at it.

Woodlice do little harm in tidy gardens, since they mostly eat decaying organic matter, and are of course vital members of the compost heap team. Occasionally they start to breed and make a nuisance of themselves around low, woody plants such as helianthemums, and in wooden barrels. If you hate them, clean up your garden. If you find them trekking across your hall, investigate for dry rot, which they also eat.

Scale insects are hard to eradicate. There are numerous different types, but the most common on outdoor plants are brown and limpet-like and are found on the stems or the backs of leaves of certain garden shrubs – bay, cornus, camellia and photinia, for example. You usually only become aware of scale insects when the infestation becomes heavy and they drip a sticky substance on to leaves below them. They can also take hold on indoor plants (look out for tell-tale sticky surfaces beneath). Indoor scale insects are tiny and vaguely orange, lurking in groups around leaf nodes and ribs.

Young scale insects are generally on the move in spring, and it is easiest to treat them then, before they develop their 'armour plating'. If I detect them quickly enough on indoor plants I use the insecticidal sticks described above (see whitefly), or I stroke them off the leaves and branches with cotton wool dipped in methylated spirits. On major outdoor shrubs, where their secretions often form an ugly black sooty coat on evergreen leaves, I think the secret is to shift as many of them as possible out of position with a gloved finger or hand to loosen them, and then spray the entire bush with a systemic/contact insecticide while they are exposed and vulnerable. You can try washing evergreens with a dilute solution of washing-up liquid if the look of the sooty leaves really offends you and you have time for such housewifely gardening.

Capsid bugs is the name given to a group of long-leggedy beasties that move so fast they are hardly ever seen, but can be devastating to many herbaceous plants and late-flowering shrubs, notably fuchsia and caryopteris. They nibble at developing shoots and flower buds, injecting via their 'saliva' a substance that destroys plant cells. When the affected shoots unfold, they are puckered and dotted with tiny holes and the whole nasty episode can result in a total lack of blooms. By the time the disfigurement is seen, the beasts will have legged it elsewhere (to overwinter in your hedges, probably – they favour hawthorn). If you have a problem one year, the next year you can spray susceptible plants preventatively with a systemic spray in May or June. But attacks are unpredictable – some years they are worse than others. A few plants that are messed up by capsids – notably fuchsias – can have their damaged shoot tips snipped off and they will then produce new flowering side-shoots that are undamaged.

Lily beetles are an unmissable bright scarlet, about 7mm (¼in) long, with black undersides. They nibble the petals and leaves of lilies, completely ruining them. Whenever you see them, usually in enthusiastically fornicating pairs, you should spoil their fun by picking them off the lilies and stamping on them. Park your cup of coffee first and use two hands to pick them off, since they are adept at dropping to the ground on their backs, and are then blackly invisible. Look out for their vile, slimy grubs on the leaves as well, which someone once (accurately) described to me as looking like pulsating bird-poo. Adults hibernate in the soil over winter and come out early to feast on lily relatives such as fritillaries – so you get an advance warning of their potentially devastating presence in the garden. Use a systemic insecticide preventatively. As you may have guessed from the above venomous description, I have had considerable trouble with lily beetles in my time.

Viburnum beetles are on the increase and are rapidly becoming the most reviled and difficult to tackle of all leaf pests. It is actually the larvae of the viburnum beetle that do all the damage to some (but not all) species of viburnums, emerging from eggs laid by adult beetles on the shrub's branches and nibbling tiny holes in them before making their way to the ground beneath to pupate. Systemic spraying around May will help, and again in August (there are two generations produced a year) and hard pruning may also help – although this will, of course, affect flowering for a year.

Various other larvae (the name given to offspring of insects that pupate before hatching out to become adults) are commonly troublesome. Hemerocallis gall midge, feeding inside the noticeably swollen buds of day lilies and Solomon's seal sawfly – the larvae skeletonise the foliage of Solomon's seal (*Polygonatum*) plants – are just two that spring to mind. Early spring spraying with systemic insecticide helps control them.

Vine weevils are hooked-legged, black, nocturnal beetles with long snouts. Adult weevils take characteristically regular 'U'-shaped bites from the edges of evergreen leaves as they feed (euonymus, rhododendrons and bergenias are particularly favoured). The real damage is done by their grubs, however, that hatch out from eggs laid elsewhere, frequently just beneath the surface of the compost in containers (of pansies and primulas, for example) and around the base of garden plants such as sedums and heucheras, which have especially succulent roots. Vine weevil grubs completely demolish plants. The first hint of what is going on may be when a plant wilts, and on investigation you find that you can simply lift it off the soil/compost, revealing a complete lack of roots. Investigation with an index finger will reveal numerous fat, white, curled, c-shaped grubs up to a centimetre (½in) long. The compost in the pot or soil local to the dead plant should be binned, or left on the lawn on a plastic sheet for robins to pick over.

Until fairly recently there was no way to control vine weevils effectively, and even now they often go unidentified and cause havoc to the uninitiated. In the bad old days I used to resort to going out at dead of night, holding a tea-tray under the particular rhododendron that was a known haunt of my evil weevil gang. I would bash the bush, and down would tumble the nasty nocturnal revellers. I would then run like hell with my loaded tea-tray and tip them all down the waste disposal unit in the kitchen. I would turn the 'on' switch with great gusto, having in one fell swoop interrupted the life cycle of one of my most dreaded horticultural enemies.

Thankfully these nocturnal outings are now unnecessary. No more beating about the bush, you could say, since you can control vine weevil either biologically or chemically with soil drenches (both of them helpfully called Vine Weevil Killer). The timing of treatments is all important, and detailed instructions are to be found on the packaging of the products. If you suspect you have adult weevils in the garden, it makes sense to drench the compost in all your pots routinely with one or other of the available treatments.

FUNGAL DISEASES

These tend to appear among certain susceptible plants late in the season, and can cause disfigurement and leaf drop and – if unchecked – they can, in time, kill plants. They can be treated 'organically' with copper-based fungicides, but systemic fungicides (those that are absorbed through the plant's leaves) give better results, especially if used preventatively on plants that you know are susceptible, or as soon as the first symptoms are noticed. Running a tight ship is important: picking off or clearing up fallen diseased leaves and binning rather than composting them; and keeping tools, pots and plant supports clean, so that spores do not linger. The fungal diseases you are most likely to encounter are mildews, rust and leaf spots.

Powdery mildew shows up in late summer as grey dusty leaves and tends to occur on plants that are dry at the roots and grown in cramped conditions, with little air circulation. Certain perennials, notably knautia, some phlox and asters, almost always get mildew, as do some roses, particularly those grown in dry soil at the base of hot walls. Plants that get mildew one year will certainly get mildew the next – so a preventative spray with systemic fungicide may well be necessary. Mulching around likely candidates in spring to retain moisture in the soil helps too.

Downy mildew (botrytis) is altogether different, and is a result of soggy, often humid conditions – furry white mould on clusters of flowers and leaves, and blackening rotting stems are all too familiar symptoms. Cut off and bin affected parts and then spray the rest of the plant. As a precaution, seedlings can be drenched with a special fungicide formulated for the purpose to prevent 'damping off' – a term used where botrytis wipes out whole trays of the poor things almost overnight.

Rust is perhaps most commonly seen on the leaves and stems of hollyhocks, which become horridly disfigured by small orange blisters. Rust is spread via spores that linger on the soil below the plants and are splashed upwards by rain. If you don't want to use a systemic fungicide (which does in fact prevent and control rust quite well), you have to work hard to keep these short-lived plants looking good, especially as they age. Remove all spotty lower leaves that appear early in the season and from then onwards strip any damaged leaves off the stems as they power upwards. (Or you can chuck them every other year and start again.)

Fungal leaf spots is a vague description given to a whole host of nasties with similar symptoms – black spots that develop on older leaves, which then yellow and fall. The one we know best is rose black spot, but there are other woody plants that suffer similarly – photinia and some hebes, as well as herbaceous plants such as pansies and primulas. Hard to control, at least each is specific to its host (by which I mean that rose black spot will not spread to your primulas or the other way around). Systemic fungicides give a little control, but spraying will need to be repeated.

VIRUSES

Unlike fungal diseases, the numerous viruses that can affect plants are incurable. They generally cause puckering, stunting and mottling of leaves. Most gardeners try treating odd and unidentified ailments such as those described with fungicide. By all means have a go, but if there is no improvement, the only sensible thing you can do is dig up the plant and burn it. Sap-sucking insects spread viruses, so an obvious precaution is to take great care to prevent aphid attacks on particularly vulnerable plants, notably clematis and lilies. All very depressing, I am sure you agree, so we will move on.

SOME DOS AND DON'TS ON HOW TO USE FUNGICIDES AND INSECTICIDES SAFELY AND EFFECTIVELY

If you have not already got one, get a small 1.25-litre (2-pint) pump-spray bottle. You should, however, always remember the following:

Don't mix up too much solution (hence my advice that you should only get a small pump-spray bottle). Once mixed up, fungicides – that kill fungal diseases and blights – and insecticides (you understand that one), cannot be stored, unlike the ready-to-use ones you can buy, which are formulated to have a long shelf life. If you mix up too much solution, you will be tempted to use the excess where it is not strictly necessary or tip it down the domestic drain system, which is a no-no. You should, in fact, pour any excess mixture on to waste ground and wash it away with additional water.

Don't spray in strong sunshine, high winds, or near ponds, pets and, of course, children.

Don't forget to wear some protection for your skin, and wash thoroughly after you have finished. No one realistically expects gardeners to don a full spacesuit to spray a couple of roses, but wearing gloves and long-sleeved and long-legged clothing, and, if you can bear it, a mask, is a sensible practice.

Don't go looking for trouble. As I have said before, small, intensively planted gardens, especially those in towns, do get very pest- and disease-ridden. The lack of winter frost and sharp cold winds ensure that certain spores hang around and pests can be active virtually all the year round. However, there is a natural balance in nature, a sort of 'bug-eat-bug' situation. You can upset this balance easily so that a pest becomes a plague if you knock out all its natural predators. So try to turn a blind eye to minor horrors unless they disfigure your plants and garden unbearably.

Don't career round the garden too often, Rambo-style, with a bottle loaded up with killer-gunk on the 'just in case' basis.

Do try to use all your garden sprays in the evening – for two reasons. Bees will be less active, and the insecticide or fungicide will remain damp on the surface of leaves for longer, thereby ensuring maximum absorption by the plant.

Do seek out and use systemic products (ones that enter the plant through leaves or sometimes roots, and make plants more resistant to disease and unpalatable to pests). The effects of these chemicals last far longer than with purely contact sprays (though generally not as long as the manufacturers claim) and in the case of insecticides, in addition to killing off breeding adults, you clobber most of the next generation of each pest as well. With contact sprays, you have to almost literally hit each bug in the eye, and drenching every leaf on each side is an unrealistic aim.

Do, therefore, learn as much as you can about the life cycle of your known and previously experienced enemies. Systemic sprays act best if they are used preventatively, so spraying a plant *before* it is visited by a nibbler or egg-layer is often the secret of success. Horses, stable doors and all that.

Do use the recommended doses – follow instructions on the packaging *to the letter*. Making up an 'extra-strong' solution can harm your plants.

Do run a tight ship. Clear away blighted leaves, bag up or burn all nasty bits, and every so often clear up old stacks of plant pots and the bits behind the shed that you would rather not look at. Heaven forbid that I should encourage anyone to be one of those gardeners who spend whole weekends hoovering the borders and power-jetting the patio, but a little sensible tidiness goes a long way towards creating a less pesty environment.

WEEDS

Some of us really care about weeds, others really don't. It is, of course, a matter of scale. Many large and posh country gardens are awash with ground elder. The owners probably don't turn a hair and indeed it is probably hardly noticeable in the grand scheme of things. In smaller gardens weeds may be a different matter entirely. Nothing goes unnoticed, every leaf is fussed over and the obliteration of even the most mild-mannered weed can become an obsession. I had a husband years ago who was obsessed with what I call 'the London weed' – oxalis. Not the most delicate-footed, he would trample whole borders, even on one occasion smashing a precious delphinium (actually our garden was tiny, and had only one 'border' – which made his misdemeanour all the worse), in order to reach clusters of this annoying little intruder.

A lot depends, of course, on how you define the term 'weed'. Those blasé big-garden people will, in fact, snap into action with a fork or bottle of weedkiller if the ground elder flowers humiliatingly in the middle of some highly prized perennials, or the bindweed surprises them with a jovial floral wave from the top of an apple tree. (There is too much to do, they will tell you archly. You can't afford the time to get picky about things like weeds in the country.)

But for most of us, you could say that a weed is any plant that invades the territory of other, more delicate ones, spoiling the way they look and threatening their existence. Even something as gentle and pleasant as that lovely, papery, pale-yellow Welsh poppy can be seen as a weed if it overwhelms your alpines; but if it gently infiltrates the cracks between some shady paving stones beneath sombre trees where little else will grow, it could be viewed as a bit of a bonus, a plant to be encouraged, even.

So what can you do if you have an embarrassment of interlopers or are – go on, admit it – a fully fledged weedophobe?

Two useful rules to remember

One of the first rules you should make for yourself is *never let a real weed*

157

flower, for obvious reasons. So, at the first sight of a bold yellow dandelion, rip off its head. You can deal with the rest of the plant later. If the dandelion has already formed a 'clock', crunch the head in the palm of your hand as you grasp it and dispose of it carefully, or it will release its seeds to the wind. (Garden neurotics may well find themselves, an hour or so later, trying to fasten a rose tie or open a fertiliser packet still clutching a clammy paw full of such treasures, having totally forgotten what it is in their hand and why it is there, but still holding on for grim death anyway).

The NLRWF rule is a bit of a hard one to stick to if, for example, you regard prolific seeders like forget-me-nots or the aforementioned Welsh poppy as weeds. In this event, you may want to enjoy the flowers, but then have to stop them dropping their seeds everywhere, which means you have to be quick off the mark after they have flowered, either pulling the whole plant out of the ground (forget-me-nots) or dead-heading them with a passion (poppies).

Incidentally, if your forget-me-nots are only a problem because they are in the *wrong* place, pull them up very gently just as they are going to seed, and shake them upside down in the *right* place, and hey presto. You can do this with all sorts of self-seeders.

The second rule is to familiarise yourself with your weedlings. Learn to recognise bogeymen when they are mere bogeybabies, when eradication is far easier. I am thinking here of really loony weeds such as dock, thistles, that borage-like blue-flowered hairy thing called alkanet (so many of us nurture these thinking they are foxgloves, but *feel* the difference: only if it is silky is it a foxglove) and any dandelions that manage to slip through your net. If you recognise them early, you can whip them out with no trouble. If you miss them and they get their roots down deep, your weed obliteration programme moves into a whole different league.

Annual weeds

Weed seeds of all kinds can lie dormant in the soil for years, germinating only when they are offered the right combination of light, moisture, warmth and so on. While it is easy to assume that weeds are a spring and summer problem, some of the most irritating annual weeds such as hairy bittercress and chickweed may flower and set seed most of the year.

If your garden has suffered from years of neglect, the chances are your topsoil is full of dormant seeds just waiting to snap into action and torment you. It makes sense in these circumstances, if you are planning a major planting project, to wait a few weeks after your initial purge and soil preparation. Let the first generation of weed seeds you have brought to the surface germinate, and either hoe them or hand-weed them, disturbing the soil as little as possible. The longer you leave the area alone before you plant, the more weeds you will be able to destroy this way. A weed-smothering mulch – at least 5cm (2in) deep, more if you can – applied after you have done your new planting will help keep the lid on things thereafter.

HOW TO WEED

There is a knack to both hoeing and hand-weeding:

Always hoe on a sunny, breezy day if at all possible, so that disturbed seedlings instantly wilt and die, rather than simply re-rooting and carrying on.

Always use both hands when hand-weeding – a small hand fork in one, a glove on the other: roots of many weeds (chickweed is the worst offender) snap off at ground level and they simply re-grow.

Perennial weeds

The worst and most common of these are without doubt ground elder and bindweed, with that tiny aforementioned irritant oxalis not far behind.

Ground elder
Ground elder is a cow-parsley relation with invasive but fairly shallow roots that spread rapidly if you let them, quickly invading the bases of clumpy border plants. Every snapped-off piece of root is capable of re-generating, becoming a new plant within weeks. You can use Glyphosate (see pages 161–2) on isolated patches of ground elder. Make sure it is in full leaf, and water it to 'plump it out' before you use the weedkiller. But once ground elder has invaded other plants there is nothing for it but to dig them up, pull out the white roots of the evil interloper (working from the underside of each one), before replanting them in thoroughly dug-over and cleansed soil. Large infested areas should be completely 'gutted', the cleansed, wanted plants potted up temporarily while the bare ground is left fallow – however meticulous you are, scraps of the weed will always show up and can be winkled out before they, too, become hooligans.

Bindweed
A familiar hedgerow twining climber, bindweed is similarly invasive. It also has vividly white roots, but they lie far deeper in the ground and if anything snap and re-grow more easily, making this particular monster virtually impossible to eradicate by simply digging. Most gardeners I know resort to using Glyphosate on bindweed. There are all sorts of rather gimmicky tricks you can use, but possibly the best involves encouraging the emerging shoots to grow up tall canes (instead of twining, for example, into shrubs), then sliding the growth down the cane and spritzing it with the weedkiller, using a cut-off drinks bottle as an isolating barrier.

Oxalis
This group of attractive low-growing plants with shamrock-like leaves are an extreme irritant to obsessive tidy-freaks. While they don't throttle other plants, they are all somewhat invasive. The worst (*O. corymbosa*) grows from little green-ish bulbs that it is possible to lift out of the soil carefully using a kitchen fork – as long as you get at them before midsummer, after which the bulbs become dry and shatter into a million soil-coloured bulbils if disturbed, spreading the whole problem far and

wide. Weedkillers are pretty ineffective. Try to get rid of oxalis if you must, then please, please give up and go and get a life.

Serious ground clearing

If you have the time and patience, it really is a good idea to cover weedy ground with black plastic (thus excluding light and water from the area you want to cultivate in the future), leaving it in situ for as long as you can bear to – but at least six months. Perennial weeds will eventually give up and annual weeds will try to germinate and die – and quite a lot of the 'seed bank' in the soil will be baked to death in the pretty intense heat that builds up underneath the plastic when the sun shines. I managed to create an immaculate weed-free veg garden out of a former patch of lawn in this way.

The main fly in the ointment proved to be what seemed to be an extended family of moles that thought it was a tropical holiday camp and moved in for a worm-fest under the plastic. Evicting them when the time came to remove the plastic was not easy. Or alternatively you can simply use Glyphosate. (I have done this, too, in order to convert another piece of ground into a border in double-quick time.) If you are tackling a general jungle rather than just grass and weeds, you have to trawl over it thoroughly first to see if there are plants you want to save. Pot them up and grow them for a few weeks or months in large containers while you knobble the rogues, by determined digging, Glyphosate, black plastic or a combination of all three.

What about weedkillers?

I have, over the years, had a bit of a change of heart about weedkillers. I was never a fan of the powerful scorched-earth-policy things that have now almost all been banned and really had not much use for them anyway, when I started out as a town gardener. I have since taken to occasionally using weedkillers based on Glyphosate to clobber perennial weeds quickly and easily. Glyphosate acts when it comes in contact with greenery – *any* greenery, so you have to use it very carefully and protect (with upturned buckets or bin bags) any plant(s) nearby that you want to keep.

Glyphosate starts acting immediately, taking about two weeks to work its way downwards to kill roots of even tough perennials. It then breaks down in the soil (so you can plant or replant as soon as the treated weeds have died), and thus does not travel and affect neighbouring plants. There are ready-mixed Glyphosate products useful for isolating and spritzing tiny infestations, as well as super-strength ones for killing ivy and tree stumps. With the toughest perennial weeds, one application may not be enough but you should wait until the maimed weeds have re-grown enough to give you as large a leaf surface as possible before you repeat the treatment. It may be worth mentioning that Glyphosate is the only chemical weedkiller that is acceptable to *some*, but not all, organic gardeners.

You can also buy weedkillers that combine Glyphosate with other powerful chemicals that, used in spring, inhibit all seed germination for several weeks (useful, therefore, for clearing drives and paths), as well as those that are selective (used by lawn perfectionists to kill weeds and moss but not grass). While all modern weedkillers sold to gardeners have, by law, to be 'safe' for children and pets to walk and play on once they are dry, they should all be handled with the utmost care and caution. And in the unlikely event that I should take up obsessive lawn care as a hobby, and if I possessed such a thing, I wouldn't let my pet bunny graze treated areas.

Final words
Always, *always* follow manufacturers' instructions to the letter – even write down a list of recommended dilutions on a piece of paper and pin it on the inside of the shed door. Also re-read the list of dos and don'ts above. Acquire a red watering can if you are going to use weedkillers extensively, or buy a spray bottle and dedicate it purely to weed killing. Terrible things can happen to your garden if you ignore either of these bossy bits of advice.

CHAPTER 9

Propagation without a greenhouse, for the hitherto disinclined

Some gardeners take to plant propagation like ducks to water. Natural nurturers, they live with a constant array of little pots of this and that littered around on every available hard surface, outside and in. Infuriatingly for the rest of us, all they seem to have to do to create a myriad cuttings is to poke lifeless stumps of haphazard prunings and trimmings into pots of ropey old soil and, hey presto, the next minute – trees. Worse still, they propagate plants successfully on cluttered kitchen windowsills in algae-filled jam jars that look like the dippings from primordial swamps. There seems to be no stopping these people, except that they tend already to have completely stuffed gardens with nowhere to display the results of their overdeveloped talents. So what do they do? They press their ugly little charges into our hands. And *we* kill them.

This chapter is about laid-back propagation for normal mortals, for the average, busy 'killer gardeners' who have as yet to manage to grow even a broad bean in a jam jar successfully (remember school?), but who hanker after a few old-fashioned sweet peas, perhaps, or would like to take a cutting of a friend's unusual pelargonium, or maybe who need to divide a huge clump of something ordinary that has got a bit big in the border. So, no mist propagation systems, no greenhouse shading or sterilisation (probably no greenhouse even). No leaf cuttings or complicated grafting. No growing rare and temperamental orchids from seed. Just very basic propagation, getting a few new plants for almost nothing.

PLANT DIVISION

This is the simplest way to increase your stock of plants, and provides 'swapping material' with which to ply other gardeners. It is simplicity itself, particularly with clump-forming herbaceous perennials, such as hardy geraniums, all those vigorous border daisies and so on. If a plant gets too big for its boots, and preferably before it begins to weaken in the middle as a result, you dig it up and divide it into smaller sections – one of which can be replanted at the original site, and the rest can be planted elsewhere or potted up and given away.

If you are dividing a really old clump, throw away the middle section and just keep the outer edge growth. As long as there is a healthy bit of root and a healthy shoot or two on each piece you retain, everything will be fine. Replant, adding plenty of organic stuff to the soil to give the new plantlets a fresh start. If you are potting up bits for friends, it goes down well and looks a bit more professional if you plant them in some decent soil-based compost such as John Innes No. 2 rather than your own garden soil, which will inevitably sprout a large population of weedlings as soon as your back is turned, thereby damaging your reputation as a fastidious gardener.

The mechanics of division

I have been frequently amused by the number of garden hacks and television wallahs who assume that we all have two garden forks to insert neatly back to back into the middle of overgrown clumps of plants in order to divide them. I am sure this is the ideal way to tease apart massive root systems if, in addition to possessing two forks, you also have five-foot-long arms and biceps like a shot-putter. In reality, for most of us, dividing large herbaceous clumps involves just one fork, one welly, an inelegant manual tussle and some doubtful language.

Some smaller plants such as primulas, which have fibrous roots, can be relatively easily teased apart by hand, the separate new plantlets being quite obvious. Others seem to have steel girders built into their roots, and plants such as hostas or day lilies have to be divided by being chopped quite savagely with a spade or, for the more lily-livered among us, cut up using an old bread knife perhaps.

When to do it

The refinement of this job is knowing what prefers to be divided when. Early autumn and spring are the traditional times for the division of clumps, but some plants react adversely if divided just before the winter. The aforementioned primulas will be happy if they are divided in the autumn, while those chopped-up hostas will grow away more quickly if they are divided in spring when their nose-like shoots are just about to push up through the soil.

As a general rule, I feel more comfortable about dividing in the spring those herbaceous plants that totally disappear underground during deepest winter. You are less likely to forget where they are if you

replant them just as they are about to shoot upwards. Plants that do not die back completely, maintaining their presence by keeping a rosette of leaves or some other evidence of life during the winter, I am happy to divide in the autumn. Of course, it all depends on the circumstances. If you are doing major work to an entire border, you just have to get on with dividing things up and replanting whatever time of year it is and hope for the best. The moral of the tale is that you should always put marker sticks or labels into the soil where you replant things. We all think we will remember where things are, but in the hurly-burly of our thrilling gardening lives, we usually forget.

Dividing irises

Irises – the ones with the ugly, gnarled rhizomes that look like old gardeners' fingers – must be divided and replanted if they have become congested and have stopped flowering well, and this is a job best tackled around July. You have to dig up the entire clump, throw away the worst, unproductive bit in the middle, and keep the outermost 'fingers', each with a root end and a shoot end. Replant these almost horizontally (sprinkle some bonemeal on the new site first) without covering them with soil, about 23cm (9in) apart, with the shoot end pointing north. This is not as barmy as it sounds: the rhizomes need full summer sun to form the next year's flower buds, so they must not be shaded by their own leaves to any great extent. Make sure therefore that the new site is really sunny.

Spreading themselves far and wide

Some herbaceous plants, instead of making larger and larger clumps, start to run around the border by sending out suckers or runners. These are often thought to be seedlings but, in fact, are joined to the original plant by long roots. In the main, plants that run are an utter nuisance (think of garden mint) and, if they are not checked, can turn a carefully planned mixed border into mixed wilderness in a couple of seasons. However, you can sever a few errant bits of this and that (the cut stems will quickly make new roots of their own) and pot them up to give away to your worst enemy. Conversely, I should look sideways, if I were you, at any 'friend' who offers you *Achillea ptarmica* 'The Pearl', *Euphorbia cyparissias* or *Artemisia pontica* (try growing this one in a pot, which is how it looks best).

Runaway garden hooligans can very occasionally be fun. In my London garden I enjoyed a great on/off affair with that colossus of the border, *Macleaya cordata*, with its man-sized stems and huge glaucous leaves and madly suckering habit. My neighbour and I sent it to and fro under our fence between our gardens for several years. One year she had it, the following year she would wage war on it and what was left would run next door to me. The next year, I would do the same, and so it went on.

Other border plants and ground-cover plants spread by means of runners (like wild strawberry plants that usefully grow in shade), new little plants being produced from a bud at the end of each shoot. All you need to do is peg the shoot down in a little pot of compost sunk into the ground near the 'mother' plant. When the new plant is produced, you can sever the shoot and you have a small potted plant to grow on, give away or plant somewhere else.

Dividing bulbs and corms

Bulbs (daffodils, tulips, alliums) and corms (crocus, crocosmia) can be divided or congested clumps thinned out to increase your stock. But here, risking the wrath of the parsimonious, I tend to draw the line. Unless the bulbs or corms in question are, for example, the only specimens in the northern hemisphere and were brought back from a remote corner of the Transvaal by a famous gardener in his or her sponge bag as a special, special present, then I would not bother.

If you remove the small bulbs, called offsets, that you often see attached to daffodil bulbs, they will not flower for a year or two, so if you want more daffodils it is probably easier and quicker to go and buy some. If bulbs or corms stop being productive it may be that it is their growing conditions (lack of light or water), not merely congestion, that is the cause of the problem. It might be better to heave them out and replant them elsewhere.

167

Most bulbs and corms – sold loose or in packets – cost considerably less for a good few than a bunch of flowers from the supermarket. If they are so very expensive, should you be spending that much anyway on a pretty vulnerable and chancy form of plant life in the hands of the average gardener, however zealous? And if you disagree, go and read a proper detailed propagation book, which will perhaps convince you that there are some things – such as dividing bulbs, growing shrubs, trees or things like agapanthus or wisteria from seed – that are just not worth the effort for normal mortals. Which brings me on to...

GROWING FROM SEED INDOORS

This is an area that can provide us with a lot more fun than the rather worthy and sensible area of plant division. You can grow yourself all sorts of little annual flights of fancy on even the slimmest of windowsills if you are of a mind to do so, provided you read the instructions on the seed packets and follow some very simple rules.

You can, of course, even grow perennials and biennials by starting them from seed indoors, planting them out when they are small and watching them carefully as young transplants until they mature. For all sorts of reasons this can be a tricky business and if you are a true beginner I think it helps to start with annuals that have large seeds, to give you as near to instant gratification as you can get from propagation. You can just plant two or three seeds to a pot at the appropriate time, cover them with a bit of clingfilm until germination, and keep an eye on them for the first weeks or so until they make their first true leaves (the ones that resemble their adult leaves). You will need to thin the seedlings down to one per pot (see guidelines on pages 170–71) by taking out the puniest and even moving the best ones on into their own pots of John Innes No. 2 for a few weeks before you plant them out with, therefore, minimal root disturbance.

Ideal for starters

The plants I usually recommend to first-time seed growers are quick annual climbers because, being large, the seeds are easy to handle, and you get a lot of growth and flower drama for the amount of effort you put in. I particularly recommend *Cobaea scandens*, canary creeper (and other nasturtiums), *Ipomoea* (morning glory), or some of the more interesting sweet peas. Try 'Cupani', for example, the maroon and purple 'original' sweet pea, since the little pots of seedlings that you can buy 'off the peg' from virtually every flower shop or greengrocer you pass in early spring are usually bog-standard varieties.

I have had great success growing annual climbers in fibre growing tubes, packed tightly side by side in old 2-litre plastic pots and filled with a sand/multi-purpose compost mixture or loam-based John Innes No. 1. The advantage of these tubes, which are quite cheap to buy, is that they are tall and slim, encouraging the formation of deep roots that climbers like to make. Being biodegradable, the whole caboodle is planted in the soil and there is, therefore, virtually no check to the young plant's growth.

Sowing smaller seeds

If you are more confident and a bit more ambitious, you could try to grow herbs such as coriander or basil – which you will have to sow at intervals during the summer since they go to seed or get picked and eaten very quickly. Or you could try some big annuals such as cosmos, cleome and *Nicotiana affinis* (big white tobacco plants) mentioned earlier. Some of these present little problem since the seeds are quite manageable, and you can plant them two or three to a pot or growing tube and thin them out.

Nicotiana is a different story. The seeds are like dust, and it is well nigh impossible to sow them thinly. The answer is to mix them with a little fine dry sand – sandpit sand will do – which not only 'dilutes' them, but also makes it possible to see where you have sprinkled them. All the same they will be very congested when they come up and will have to be ruthlessly culled unless you want to end up with every windowsill in the house covered with sad, stringy, lolling seedlings in little pots that need watering at least twice a day.

Some basic guidelines for growing from seed indoors without a greenhouse

1 The most important rule of all: don't grow too much of one thing. 'Pricking out' – the official term for thinning – dozens of seedlings like they do in proper greenhouses is for serious gardeners. It is far, far easier to sow little potfuls of things, with just a few seeds in each. Thin out ruthlessly and chuck seedlings away if you germinate too many.

2 Use fibre pots packed in old plastic plant pots, or special propagation packs – clear, plastic domes over trays with individual cells in which to plant seeds, which make handling the plants simpler. Some propagators are conveniently windowsill shaped – longer and narrower.

3 Use proper seed-growing compost. I use John Innes No. 1 or alternatively a mixture of multi-purpose compost with some fine sand added. Make sure that whatever you use has had all the lumps rubbed out of it so that it has a fine texture, and that it is well saturated and drained *before* you sow your seeds. You could drench the compost with a fungicide to prevent the seedlings going mouldy (known as 'damping off') in the early days. There are copper-based fungicides for use by organic gardeners, as well as inorganic ones developed specially for use on edible crops.

4 Sow seeds as thinly as possible on the damp compost and cover them with dry compost. Big seeds with hard cases, such as morning glory, should be soaked overnight beforehand. Remember that seeds need to be covered by their own 'height' of soil. Half-inch seeds need half an inch of compost on top, grains-of-sand-sized seeds need the merest sprinkling of compost on top.

Do not water the pots again until the seeds have germinated or the seeds may get washed about.

5 If you are not using a little propagator, cover the pots of seed with clingfilm until germination. Keep them out of the sun.

6 Once the seeds have germinated, remove the clingfilm or open the vents on the propagator lid. Seedlings need a lot of light, which is where the problems start. The seedlings will get tall and skinny if they get too little light, and may dry out and die if they get too hot. If they are still in a covered propagator, they can easily get too warm and damp, and then go mouldy. You have to check on them at least once a day to make sure that all is well.

7 If you are growing a few seeds in each pot, remove the weakest ones to allow the big ones to expand, and eventually separate the two or three biggest and grow them in individual pots in stronger compost, such as John Innes No. 2.

8 When you have to handle seedlings in order to transfer them to bigger pots, pick them up by their leaves, not their stems, and use a kitchen fork to loosen their roots. Make a wide hole in the new compost pot with a pencil end, lower the delicate little roots in very carefully and water in with a few drops of water from a spoon. Once transplanted, seedlings will take several days to get over the shock and start growing again.

9 Harden off young plants properly by giving them a gentle transition into the outside world. Put them outside, out of the sun and wind at first, during the day and bring them in at night, for a week or so. Spring may appear to have sprung and the daytime temperatures may be quite high, but for these little chaps it is night-time temperature and soil temperature that are of crucial importance. If you take little plants off a windowsill and plunge them into the cold ground without this period of acclimatisation, not only will the new leaves go very pale and be unable to grow, but the existing flimsy leaves, unused to direct sunlight, will probably scorch. Either way, you could find you have wasted a lot of time and energy.

10 Finally: I cannot stress enough the need to hold off as long as

possible on the sowing of seeds indoors, where the atmosphere is dry and warm and the daylight on offer less than full, even on a windowsill. Climbers in particular grow like the wind once they get going, and can soon outgrow any pathetic support you may have to give them (knitting needles and kebab sticks have both been spotted not a million miles from here) before the weather is genuinely warm enough for them to be planted outside so they can ramp away unchecked.

GROWING ANNUALS FROM SEED OUTDOORS

At some time or other in our gardening past, most of us have succumbed to the fantasy that you can chuck a few seeds on bare earth and get miraculous results. Indeed you frequently see packets and cartons of seeds on the market tantalisingly called things like 'Cottage Garden Mixture', 'Butterfly Mixture', 'Scented Garden Mixture', that overtly tempt us into this method of gardening. The problem with growing things from seed outside is that few of us have anything like weed-free soil, and this alone makes it difficult to avoid ending up nurturing a small patch of mixed weeds until it is, humiliatingly, too late.

I am afraid the answer to this problem would seem to be to shun all the glamorously named seed mixtures and to sow patches of one thing clearly marked with little name labels, and to grow things in strict rows – which is something weeds conveniently never do.

How to do it

To sow, you make little channels called drills with the end of a stick. Dribble a little water along the bottom of each drill, space the seeds out along them and flick the dry soil back into the drill over the seeds. Do not plant the seeds too deeply (see guideline no. 4, page 170), and keep the area moist once the seedlings appear by watering with a very fine rose on a watering can. If you have a cat, cover the area loosely with a piece of chicken wire since all cats will naturally assume that a smooth piece of soil has been created especially for them to sleep in, or worse.

Once the seeds have all come through the soil, start thinning them out so that they have room to grow. Don't even think about transplanting the thinnings, it just doesn't work. The eventual spacing of the plants will be indicated on the seed packet. If you don't thin out your seedlings in accordance with the instructions, you will get small and overcrowded plants that won't do very well. In my own experience it is this reluctance to thin seedlings out that is responsible for the greatest failures.

What looks good on television...

Only at the behest of a television producer have I ever planted one of those borders consisting almost *entirely* of annuals, where you mark out areas with lines of sand, planting different seeds in each patch. This is just not my personal style of gardening, since it involves far too much bare earth and far too much fiddling around in late spring. It does work after a fashion, but to prevent such a volume of juicy annual growth collapsing in a rainstorm and becoming a complete mess, you need to be able to get into it and provide some sticks-and-string support, which is extremely difficult to do. And again, you run the risk of ending up with a large colony of willowherb or sow thistle suddenly flowering gamely just beyond your reach in the middle of it all.

At the end of the season you have to pull it all up. You are thus back to square one again with all that naked soil, and you have very little to show for all the effort you put in. To my mind this is not good for morale. Alas, there is a vast difference between what looks good on television and what makes for satisfying gardening in real life.

Sowing hardy annuals and biennials outside in late summer

Most of the plants we grow as bedding plants will not self-seed in our climate, with its short growing season. I have in recent years had unexpected appearances late in the summer of self-sown tobacco plants, lobelia and even cosmos, but it is not something you can take for granted. However, if left to their own devices, certain annuals known as 'hardy annuals' will deposit their seeds around in late summer when they will instantly germinate, survive as small seedlings through all but the most atrocious of winters, growing on and flowering early in the following summer. In my garden I have colonies of such great border standbys as blue love-in-the-mist (*Nigella*), and 'Mother of Pearl' poppies (also known as 'Fairy Wings') and even a few plants of the once highly fashionable inky-blue *Cerinthe major* show up here and there, all of which can survive on this basis and are invaluable.

Establishing colonies of annuals

You can start off a self-perpetuating colony by imitating nature and sowing seeds of hardy annuals randomly in a border in August or September. As long as you teach yourself to recognise the seedlings, you will get results the following summer. Even if you don't do so at first, and inadvertently weed some of them out or disturb them, some seedlings are bound to escape your ignorant rampaging and will prosper – probably in the most unlikely places and with interesting results.

The following spring the foliage of these junior hardy annuals should be stout enough to be recognisable as something important (love-in-the-mist is distinctively feathery and quite un-weed-like), so you can thin them out or isolate them into good-sized clumps. The thinnings can be replanted, but they will not grow as big and gutsy as the undisturbed plants, and will flower later.

You should deadhead hardy annuals sparingly, just enough to encourage continued flowering while keeping some old flowers to form seed. It is no great hardship to live with – the seedheads of my love-in-the-mist and poppies have a charm of their own. With a bit of luck they will self-seed year after year. This is just the sort of gardening I love.

Sowing biennials

Biennial seeds can also be cast around in midsummer in the hope that some of them will imitate nature and turn up as viable plantlets the following year, to flower two summers hence. In my experience, sowing biennials this way is a bit of a long shot, as the likelihood of person-sown seed falling on suitable ground and coming through two seasons without mishap is slim. I am thinking here particularly of foxgloves, whose dust-like seeds and minuscule seedlings seemed to have had a distinct preference for germinating only between two paving stones in the middle of an important thoroughfare in my old garden. The same plant is a certifiably lunatic weed in my new garden. Honesty seed is chunkier and has more of a chance of sensible success, and is therefore worth a try.

The answer is to sow biennials in groups in specific places. Since they transplant well after their first year's growth, they can be relocated and shoehorned into odd corners around the garden to look 'natural'. This bit of well-planned artifice is practised by numerous gardeners, and works a treat.

SHRUB PROPAGATION – LAYERING AND TAKING CUTTINGS

To many gardeners, taking cuttings is what proper propagation is all about. They see it as a challenge, to persuade, by various means, all sorts of plants to produce roots from unexpected places – stems or sometimes shoot-tips, or even leaves.

My own success with cuttings is, I freely admit, patchy, and my excuses vary depending on how defensive I feel about it. Generally I claim that my lack of zeal and/or success has a lot to do with the fact that for most of my gardening life I have been a gardener with an exceedingly stuffed small garden, offering me little incentive to take cuttings of shrubs. Also, when I started out I had keen gardener parents who pressed their surplus cuttings into my ever-open hands. I had, as many of us do, a crowded, sill-less, centrally heated house, making it hard to succeed with anything that needed protection from the elements. When I tried things out, I attempted to do everything 'right' and yet still ended up with half a dozen cuttings of something I frankly didn't need or very much like, while the things I was really desperate to acquire died on me if I so much as took my eyes off them. I feel instinctively that I am fairly typical of today's keen but pampered gardeners.

I will, therefore, outline the principles behind the fairly complex subject of layering and taking stem cuttings. Whether or not you turn out to be a natural taker-of-cuttings is, I am convinced, in the lap of the gods.

Layering – the easier technique

Most of us will have noticed, in the course of grubbing about on our hands and knees tidying up under shrubs, that branches touching the ground often spontaneously put out roots and attach themselves to the soil. This is a shrub's natural way of propagating itself and illustrates to us gardeners the basic magic behind it all. The roots, as you will have noticed, are produced from around the point where a leaf joins a stem, called a node. Plants such as ivy (which, after all, is a shrubby climber), produce roots and shoots from just about every node that touches the ground, and special clinging roots where it touches rough, climbable surfaces.

Using a technique known as layering, you can persuade all sorts of shrubs to produce roots on branches still attached to themselves by making a small cut behind a node and pegging the branch down on to the ground each side of the cut. The soil in the immediate area can be improved with a little good compost to ensure that it retains moisture. It is a good idea to pinch out the tip of the branch, to stop it putting its energy into growing.

While slow-growing plants such as rhododendrons will take a year to get going, some shrubs put down roots this way fairly quickly: if you carry out the operation in the spring, by the end of the summer the roots should have started to grow and you can then sever the new (rather odd-shaped) plant from its 'mother'. Minimise the shock by leaving it undisturbed until the following spring, after which time it can be regarded as an independent new plant, and transplanted with care in a new site. This is probably the easiest way to propagate a wide variety of shrubs, and it is certainly worth having a go. I have even cut and pegged down branches of friends' shrubs – with their permission – and made them into surrogate propagators for me. It was very satisfying and I had far greater success with layering than I did taking proper hardwood cuttings (see pages 178–9) in my overcrowded little patch.

Suckers

Perhaps at this point I will slip in a little about propagating shrubs from suckers. I refer to shrubs such as stag's horn sumach (*Rhus typhina*). The principle of severing a shoot from the mother plant, leaving it in situ while it makes its own roots and moving it a few weeks or months later is similar to layering, in that you have to persuade a part of the original plant to make itself into an independent plant. In the case of suckers, however, you have to sever the plant from its parent first, in order to force it to make its new roots, and it is really important that you do not disturb the sucker for several months afterwards or it will just wither and die.

Sumach suckers wildly, and is often regarded as a weed. Only the female plants carry the handsome cone-like flowers in addition to having dramatic scarlet autumn leaf tints, that make it an altogether more interesting plant, worth tolerating despite its suckering habit. You can be sure of acquiring a female, of course, by taking a sucker from a female. In my experience, you rarely find female sumachs in garden centres and nurseries – you generally have to take pot luck as to their sex.

If you take suckers from shrubs that have been grafted, you will end up with a wild plant. (See rose suckers, pages 141–2.)

Stem cuttings

The most common way to propagate shrubs and many other plants is, however, by taking stem cuttings, forcing the plant to produce roots from shoots cut from them at various stages of development. As with layering, the roots are produced from the most active growing point on the stem, just below a node. Most cuttings are thus what are known as 'nodal' cuttings. However, many shrubs also respond well to what are known as 'heel cuttings', where a side shoot is torn gently from a main stem, the resulting pointed shred of bark from the main stem is trimmed neatly, and the shoot inserted into compost. Handbooks on the subject of propagation detail which shrubs respond best to each method, and if you are going into the whole propagation thing seriously you will need more information than I can provide here.

Hardwood cuttings

If you are fortunate enough to have an unused patch of ground that is sheltered, shaded at midday and not dry (not under trees, for example), you can dig in a little sand and compost to improve the soil texture and make a small cuttings bed to take hardwood cuttings of shrubs which are the slowest, but easiest, to handle.

At the end of the growing season, you should cut shoots about 30cm (12in) long from fairly stiff and brownish wood (often referred to as 'mature') that was formed in that current year. Cuts should be cleanly made just below a node, and the shoots, having had their lower leaves removed, should be stuck in the soil to the depth of about 15cm (6in).

You should reckon on about a 30 per cent success rate, so take at least six cuttings of any one variety. They will do absolutely nothing until well into the next spring and you will be convinced, by about April, that you are nurturing a graveyard. But you must absolutely resist the temptation to poke around or tweak at the little row of corpses to see if they have got roots. I write as one who knows, having impatiently pulled up many a shrivelled, perished-looking bit of vegetation only to discover little roots at the bottom. Alas, even if you shove them straight back and pretend you didn't do anything, they invariably die.

Patience will be rewarded when some, not all, of the undisturbed little twigs start to sprout new leaves. Make sure they do not dry out during the following growing season, and by the autumn you will have some free, albeit small, new plants. They are best left where they are until the spring, when they can be moved to their new homes.

Semi-hardwood cuttings

While hardwood cuttings are not generally taxing or time consuming, needing only an extraordinary degree of patience, a square metre or so of appropriately sited soil and a philosophical attitude towards failure, semi-hardwood cuttings are a completely different cup of tea.

Whatever anyone else says or writes about the subject, I must insist that it is really difficult to propagate from semi-hardwood cuttings without a) serious dedication, b) a greenhouse or a proper cold frame and c) a singular lack of desire or need for a summer holiday away from home. I cannot recommend this method of propagation to all but the fanatical few. Having stated all that, if it turns out that you are one of the lucky ones for whom any form of propagation is as simple as falling off a log, you can feel really smug.

Semi-hardwood cuttings can be taken, as the name suggests, from half-ripened (i.e. quite bendy and green), non-flowering side shoots from the current season's growth from a large variety of shrubs, generally in mid- to late summer. They root very quickly, in a matter of weeks, provided they are kept constantly humid but shaded, in a greenhouse or cold frame outdoors. Cuttings should be about 10cm (4in) long, with a straight cut just below a node and lower leaves removed. (NB Half-ripened lavender and rosemary cuttings seem to do better if they are taken as heel cuttings as described briefly above.) They should be inserted into pots of John Innes No. 1 or a mixture of sand and peat that will provide both moisture retention and good drainage.

The method of taking the cuttings is very similar to the softwood cuttings described overleaf, so please follow that. The big enemies are overheating, and the development of mould in the humid conditions, which rapidly kills the cuttings before they have a chance to root.

You can replicate the conditions of a warm, humid greenhouse by enclosing the pots of cuttings in various ways (described below), drenching the pots with a suitable fungicide and making sure that the

179

leaves of the shoots do not touch the sides of whatever it is you have used to cover them. Stand the pots outside in the shade, gradually reducing the humidity; for example, by puncturing holes in the plastic bag, if using (see opposite), as the cuttings make roots. I have succeeded on a few occasions with fuchsias using this method, but as often as not, everything goes black and furry with mould after a week or so.

A further slight discouragement arises from the fact that within a few weeks of having been put into compost, and having been the centre of so much attention and worry, the little cuttings will drop their leaves with the natural arrival of autumn. There may be no further sign of life until the spring, by which time, if you are anything like me, you will probably have lost interest in them anyway.

Softwood cuttings
I feel bad that I am passing on so much negativity about semi-hardwood cuttings, when I know that success is largely about having the right equipment and just a bit of luck.

Perhaps we should look at something a little easier: softwood cuttings. This is the name given to stem cuttings that are taken from young shoots that have not become hard or woody, and is the method used for propagating pelargoniums (often wrongly called geraniums), argyranthemums (frequently called marguerites) and a lot of the half-hardy perennials that we grow in containers. If you have a yen to try stem cuttings and you don't have space for a cuttings bed, a cold frame or a greenhouse with all the expensive gadgets and gizmos that 'pukka' gardeners have, then you should have a go at this.

Cuttings should be between 5–10cm (2–4in) long and taken from soft, fleshy main or side shoots. I find it best to cut off an entire shoot first and then take a series of cuttings from it using a craft knife and a chopping board. You can take three or four cuttings from one shoot, cutting neatly just below each leaf joint. All you need is a piece of a stem that has a node with a neat cut beneath it – each cutting does not need to have a growing tip. Pelargoniums, in particular, are very vigorous plants and you can take cuttings from them at virtually any time during the growing season. It makes sense to take a few cuttings from the shoots you remove when you cut back the lanky plants that you have over-wintered indoors in February. It also makes sense to take a few cuttings at the end of summer from those in pots outdoors that are too big to move into shelter, but will probably get nipped by a frost.

Experienced gardeners invariably find their own ways of taking softwood cuttings, and everyone will swear that their method is foolproof. A friend of mine always (successfully, of course) takes masses of softwood cuttings in supermarket meat trays filled with damp vermiculite and covered in clingfilm. (Vermiculite is a mineral-based product normally used by gardeners as a soil additive to retain moisture and air and open up soil texture.) Or she simply wedges part of a polystyrene tile into an ice-cream carton filled with water, makes holes in it and pokes little stems through them into the water. She is definitely 'one of those'. Perhaps, however, I should outline the 'textbook' version for beginners:

Fill a 2-litre plastic pot with John Innes No. 1 potting compost and make sure it is well drenched with a solution of a fungicide. Dip the cuttings in the same solution, and also dip the ends into some hormone rooting powder to help with the formation of the roots, before inserting them into the compost, about four to a pot. A propagator makes life easier, or failing that, you should make what are known as Wisley cloches for individual pots of cuttings. These are little tents made out of clear plastic bags, supported and kept away from the leaves by a couple of wire hoops inserted into the pots. Another way of making sure the cuttings stay humid is to make a 'hat' for the pot out of the top half of a clear plastic drinks bottle (with the lid on it, initially).

The cuttings should be kept out of the sun, and the humidity level kept high until evidence of root growth appears (that is, tiny leaves on the shoot). During this time the propagators or cloches will become completely steamed up, which is fine. If they are in Wisley cloches, you then reduce the humidity by cutting the corner off the plastic bag but leaving it in place for a further week or two. If they are in a plastic propagator, you can open the vent in the lid. The screw top of the drinks bottle cloche can conveniently be removed. Once the cuttings are established (two to five weeks or so, depending on the time of year), they should be potted on to a growing medium with a bit more oomph to it, such as John Innes No. 2, and feeding should start.

The last word...

There is more, much more, to propagating your own plants than I have outlined here, as you will see from even the most cursory glance at a book on the subject. I have not mentioned basal cuttings, leaf cuttings, eye cuttings, root cuttings, Irishman's cuttings, grafting and heaven knows what else. But there should be enough here to get you started. If you still think it is all rather complicated and irrelevant, next time you accidentally snap a shoot off a fuchsia or a busy Lizzie, stick it in a jar of water and see what happens. Before you know it you may find you have joined the Primordial Swamp Mob, and life may never be quite the same again.

CHAPTER 10

La batterie du jardin – some tools you seriously need, and some you seriously do not

I write this section in response to two things. Firstly, as a beginner I remember I made several mistakes and bought some useless tools. In an attempt to save money, I undoubtedly wasted a lot. Secondly, I am asked often by visitors to my garden and people to whom I give talks to recommend tools that I have found indispensable. There are so many tools and gadgets available online and on display in most garden centres that it is genuinely hard to take decisions and to sort out priorities, especially if you have never bought things for the garden before. Assaulted in the media by ads and magazine 'advertorial', it is hard to get an honest appraisal of tools anywhere. Only if you go to a good old-fashioned hardware shop to buy a saw or a screwdriver, or even a power drill, will you find someone behind the counter who has enough personal experience and know-how to point you in the right direction. The trouble with the huge garden centres and DIY superstores, where most of the gardening stuff is bought, is that there is seldom anyone there to help in quite the same way.

The difficulty in writing about tools is, of course, that they are very personal. Something that I find invaluable could be useless to someone

else. Obviously, I have not tried every gadget and gizmo on the market, although for a while I wrote a monthly tool-testing feature for a big glossy, which gave me a lot of insight. I will do my best here to list tools I think would be useful to the majority of gardeners.

SPADES AND FORKS

I hardly need say that everyone needs a spade and fork. The question is what sort.

Firstly I would say that they must be stainless steel. Once you have used stainless-steel digging tools you will understand why. They cut well, they are lighter, they don't get clogged up and heavy, except occasionally in the most appallingly heavy clay. They are more expensive than ordinary metal ones, purists will say you can't sharpen them (would any of us anyway?), but they are a lot cheaper than they used to be.

For years I used a small spade – bought for me as a birthday present doubtless because I am a small female person and it was deemed appropriate. I had a small garden, with small borders, and everything was done on a fairly small scale. As circumstances changed I started using a bigger spade. The lightness of the stainless steel means that it is not noticeably harder work to use, and when there is a large quantity of straightforward digging to do, it is definitely quicker. The small one is still brought into service for little jobs.

Forks

Actually, forks are far more important than spades, once your ground has been brought under control.

I would like to say stainless-steel forks are indestructible; however, I lent my old original to a rather large and enthusiastic New Zealander, and I think the combination of his bulk and a large underground rock got the better of it. Perhaps I should have complained to the manufacturer, but I bet there was something in the small print on the guarantee about the size of both New Zealanders and rocks. It is too late now, anyway. I replaced it with another small one: niftier than a large one when transplanting, and generally easier to get into tight corners.

HAND TOOLS

There are all sorts of wonder hand tools on the market for this or that, designed to take the hard graft out of all manner of garden drudgery. I have never managed to get on very well with weed removers, bulb planters and the like, so perhaps the advice is to try out someone else's gizmos before you buy. I have a strong suspicion that all the truly useful garden tools have already been invented, but I try not to have a closed mind about it.

Trowels and hand forks

I am sure it comes as no surprise to hear that these are totally essential, and if you have a large garden, you probably need more than one of each – one to use and one to lose. You might imagine that you can manage with just a trowel, but you really do need a small fork as well, since a fork makes hand-weeding so much easier.

Quality matters, and I am afraid there is some dreadful stuff out there – things with flowers on, pink handles and so on. In my book trowels have to be stainless steel again, since nothing else quite cuts the mustard. You can pay a lot or a little, depending on the quality of the steel, no doubt, and the type of handle. The most important thing about hand tools, particularly, is that they feel well balanced in your hand – so play around with a few before you buy.

My personal favourites are made by the Dutch company Sneeboer. The trowel is called The Ultimate Flowerbed Trowel, which just about says it all, really. It has a wooden handle that is slightly extended, and a narrow-ish curved 'blade'.

The hand fork from the same manufacturer is a winner too – quite stubby, with slightly flattened tines. I used to be wary of tools with wooden handles, but Sneeboer's seem to pass the ultimate test. I rescued one of my (two) precious hand forks from the bottom of a leaf-heap (how on earth...? no matter...), where it had been for at least a year, possibly eighteen months. It was fine. Rougher, slightly 'antiqued', but basically fine.

I have never managed to get on well with trowels or hand tools with much longer (over 35cm/14in) handles – the hand fork detailed below is an exception. In principle the idea is great, but I find them too exhausting to use. Nor do I like those hand tools with removable handles – or should that be handles with removable tools? All a bit too fussy for the likes of me.

Incidentally, brightly coloured PVC tape wrapped round the handles of small, discreetly coloured garden tools makes them easier to see, and so less likely to end up at the bottom of the compost heap.

Really long-handled little forks

These are hand forks – well, the business end is about the same size as the hand fork described above – but they have super-long handles. The one I have had for years is about 1m (3ft 3in) long overall, has a very dark-green handle (I have no idea of the manufacturer, since the label has worn off), and is incredibly lightweight. I have seen other versions that are heavier than mine, with wider tines, and they were not nearly as easy to use. Long-handled forks are invaluable for those of us with stuffed borders with minimal access, for twiddling the surface of the soil to de-compact it, to dislodge weeds that are out of reach, or to 'fiddle in' fertilisers to the top few centimetres of soil, using just a twist of the wrist. This is one of my most valued tools, and I cannot imagine gardening without it.

HOES

For some reason – memories of Mr McGregor, or our grandfathers, in well-tended vegetable gardens, perhaps – we all think we need one of these. The function of a hoe is to dislodge or decapitate weeds between plants without disturbing the soil too much (thereby avoiding activating another generation of dormant weed-seeds). I have to say that I only acquired a hoe relatively recently when I started to grow things (namely vegetables) in a weedy allotment in rows that you can hoe between. So in overstuffed flower gardens, you may find, like me, that you don't have much use for a hoe at all. I do have a small, children's hoe (i.e. narrower headed and shorter handled) that occasionally gets an airing – but not often, it has to be said.

RAKES

Rakes also belong in the vegetable garden, but have more general use in the garden, for smoothing out and tidying up areas with lumpy soil. You should never use an ordinary rake on the lawn, however, or you will rip the turf to bits.

Lawn rakes

I have always found this an indispensable tool, even when I had only a small lawn. You need to rake out the debris and dead grass from lawns in the autumn and again, more gently, in the spring. Lawn rakes are also useful for raking up leaves and other rubbish from gravel areas. Proper lawn rakes with skinny metal tines are a bit brutal for this sort of 'everyday' clearing up. Bamboo rakes with flat tines are more gentle, but don't last as long as you want them to. My absolute favourite has flat, slightly flexible plastic tines and is bright turquoise blue. One way or another it gets used almost daily.

SECATEURS

With secateurs, you get what you pay for. I have two pairs of very posh red-handled ones – Felcos, which are the Rolls Royces of secateurs and wonderful to use. I reserve these for proper pruning and keep them in leather holsters and wipe them with lubricants every so often. Then I have other ones that have seen better days, been left outside by mistake, spent time abandoned on garden walls and so on, definitely the battered Fiestas of the secateur world. I cut just about anything and everything with these and I love them to bits.

I have to say that there is an awful lot of snobbery and 'posery' attached to the choice of secateurs. If you don't do much pruning and always find yourself cutting garden wire with your secateurs, then don't buy a £40 pair just because everyone says they are the best. You neither need (nor deserve) the best, do you?

KITCHEN/GARDEN SCISSORS

I have several pairs of rough, tough, cheap (about £3 a pair) scissors that I could not do without. I do everything from opening fertiliser bags and deadheading to cutting wire with them. They are dark coloured, unfortunately, so they are frequently mislaid. Perhaps I should try to persuade someone to make them in bright colours for forgetful gardeners. The cheap IKEA ones that are bright coloured are definitely for domestic service only and are not quite strong enough for the rigours of the outdoor world, I find.

LOPPERS AND LONG-REACH PRUNERS

Two-handled loppers are a boon if you have trees and climbers that need constant attention. Judging by the number of people who have borrowed mine over the years, they are clearly not seen as a priority purchase, but I think they should be. The ones I find the easiest to use have handles that are around 65cm (2ft 2in) long.

Many two-handled loppers with telescopic handles are quite

unwieldy when extended, and more feeble operators will even find them too heavy when in short mode. My advice is to start with the lightest you can find, since trimming overhead branches is tiring even for the toughest of us.

A useful tree-pruning gadget (also borrowed by innumerable barely grateful neighbours) is my really long pruner on a telescopic pole, operated via ropes or with a sophisticated internal cord system, with a beak-like cutter on the end. Nearly everyone has overhanging trees and unreachable climbers and this really does make a difference to the chore of trying to keep them in check. In my view, with a garden full of trees, a long-reach tool like this is worth every penny you have to shell out on it.

SMALL PRUNING SAW

I have a wonderful, small, folding pruning saw with a red handle that is indispensable. It is particularly useful for getting between the thick lower stems of old roses you could not possibly cut with secateurs. Pruning saws are incredibly sharp – potentially lethal, in fact – the jagged row of 'teeth' are designed to work on the 'pull' stroke rather than the 'push'. It makes sense not to own a pruning saw that cannot be folded away, I feel, especially if there are children in the household.

GARDEN KNIFE

I have been given several garden knives in my time – indeed, it would seem to be the ideal small present for a keen gardener. My knives were natty little folding things. One of them, as I remember, even had a beautiful polished wooden handle with brass bits on it. I am ashamed to say that I have never used a garden knife, however, because I am not at all sure what they are actually for. The sort of pruning and propagating I do doesn't require the services of a knife, and for cutting twine I carry my beloved scissors or downwardly relegated secateurs with me most of the time I am out and about in my garden. I have tried hard to find a use for a garden knife, really I have. On several occasions I have slipped one into a waistcoat pocket at the start of a gardening marathon, feeling very 'Monty Don' and very proper, but have failed to find any use for it whatsoever all day. All my knives have somehow or other vanished now, probably to the great compost heap in the sky, and I doubt if I shall replace them.

BESOM (WITCH'S BROOM)

Now here is a tool no gardener should be without. It is cheap too. Besoms are invaluable for sweeping leaves off lawns, borders and rockeries without damaging plants. I used to use mine with an ordinary sweeping action, much as you would use an ordinary broom, until I saw some old gaffer doing it properly, and sweeping leaves far more efficiently as a result. You should hold the broom down low, almost horizontal to the ground, and whisk the leaves into broad heaps. You should also acquire two small pieces of plywood with which to pick up the resulting heaps. The plastic scoopers I have come across that are sold for this purpose are all far too fiddly and impossible to use if you are wearing gloves.

GLOVES

Ugh, how I used to hate them! In fact I don't know anyone who likes using gardening gloves. They make you so clumsy, prevent you from feeling what you are doing, and get wet, filthy and rigid with soil into the bargain. Yet unless you want to have hands like a navvy by the time you are thirty-five, you have to find some that will do the business. The trouble is that there are so many gardening gloves on the market, presumably to cater for every conceivable gardening need, and to fit every conceivable shape of hand. In reality, all too many of them are either made of useless and inappropriate materials for gardening or seem to have been designed to fit a curious selection of stubby-handed aliens.

After many years of trial and error, I think I have at last found gloves that just about cope with everything except the prickliest pruning jobs. The palms and fingers are made of something called nitrile (flexible and waterproof) and they have stretchy knitted backs in various weights. You can now get versions of them more or less everywhere (they were once only available via mail order or at garden shows). They are supremely comfortable and incredibly efficient – just the job for messy planting and general mucking around. The fine ones in particular fit so closely that I can really feel things through them and can even tie knots and bows with them on. They can be chucked in the washing machine when they become intolerable, or my method (a little too much information here, perhaps, about my slack domestic habits) is to do the washing-up in them – they are clean by the time I have finished!

Fed up with having almost constantly scratched arms, I have at last learned to use a pair of leather gauntlets (by Bradleys) that protect me almost up to the elbows when pruning holly hedges or sorting out tricky rambling roses. Why I didn't use them years ago, I will never know. Well actually I do know: my dislike of leather gloves stems from my early gardening days when my mother used to urge me to wear a pair of her gloves when helping her in the garden. Nasty, stiff and manky old things they were: it was about as much fun as borrowing someone else's toothbrush. At first my new gauntlets felt awkward and stiff but they quickly moulded to the shape of my hands and feel as comfortable as an old pair of slippers. I have vowed that I will never, ever offer to lend them to anyone...

Good gloves are vital, I now believe. I have finally kicked the habit of naked-handed gardening and feel as strange without a pair of gloves on out there as I do if I accidentally start my car without my seatbelt on.

TYING MATERIALS

I always have at least one ball of garden twine on the go, either green or natural coloured. (I look for 4-ply.) Twine is so often sold in those impossible old-fashioned cellophane wrappers that, once removed, reduce the ball to something resembling the regurgitation of an outsize owl that has accidentally eaten grandma's knitting bag. The secret is never to remove the packaging, and to find the end of the string in the hole in the centre of the reel, not on the outside edge (as you would on a reel of sewing cotton).

Couldn't the manufacturers of the twine supply us with cheap, unlose-able bright plastic twine holders and save us all a lot of bother? Come to think of it, the way they make the twine ensures that they must sell an awful lot more than is actually used in the garden. No point in pursuing that one, then. Alternatively, you can keep the twine on a smart oak stand, like the one I bought at one of those National Trust shops that are full of tea towels and potpourri.

I used to use twine for just about every small tying-up job in the garden, with double or even treble thickness if the situation warranted it, since it does so little harm to plant stems, making a couple of twists to act as a buffer between stems and the support to which they were tied. I generally tie things up using small bows, not knots. Although twine only lasts about a year before it has to be replaced, it is useful to have a bow you can slip undone and retie, since adjustments often have to be made mid-season.

Since this book was originally written, Flexi-Tie has hit the shelves of most garden centres. This brown reusable, hollow, tubular, soft, plastic tying material (imagine electrical flex without the wire core) is absolutely essential in my garden now. I still have uses for twine, mind you.

WATERING CANS

What on earth, you may say, can possibly be said about watering cans? *Of course* we all need one. Or two. Well, yes, we do, but there are watering cans and Watering Cans. By way of a brief digression, I will explain how in this fascinating field, the French have us knocked into a cocked hat, as the expression goes.

The design of French watering cans, which have single handles that arch over from the base to the top in line with the spout, is such that you can carry and use them one with one hand. Instead of being round, as you might expect, the cans are oval in profile, so that they don't knock your legs as you walk and slop water into your slippers. As you carry them, your hand is in the same position as if you were carrying a suitcase. Your other hand is, therefore, free to carry your breakfast coffee or your pre-prandial tipple, or if you really mean business, a pair of secateurs or a trowel.

Watering cans of the traditional two-handled British design, however, are cumbersome and cylindrical in shape, and have to be carried by the top handle with your hand unnaturally crooked forward, ape-style. When they are heavy and full, you have to hold both handles to enable you to pour from them. Anything else you are trying to carry must therefore be tucked into a pocket, held between the teeth or put down (and lost).

I find it fascinating that such a basic bit of garden equipment should be so different – and so much better – on the other side of the Channel, since I always thought that the British were supposed to be the great gardeners. I decided to look into the matter further and unearthed the fact that at some time in the past, we and the French apparently 'swapped' designs because we preferred each other's watering cans. How perverse is that? I am happy to say, however, that cheap plastic watering cans imported in thousands from the Far East are almost all made in the 'French' style (because they are simpler and probably cheaper to mass-produce).

On a more practical note, a watering can of any nationality holding more than 10 litres (about 2 gallons) is too heavy for most of us. I find several smaller cans more useful than one large one. I also like cans with really long spouts (like my small galvanised, very British, Haws can), as well as another slimline, one-handled can, the Nu-Can – which has a push button in the handle so that you can precisely target where, and how much water you deliver.

On the subject of watering, I do recommend getting a hose reel for your hose. For small gardens the new automatically non-scrambling retractable ones look like a godsend if you can bear to spend so much money on such an intrinsically boring item. I have mentioned elsewhere the lance attachment that makes it so easy to water things out of reach, delivering as softly as rainwater, just as if the hose were a watering can. I love this gadget so much that it deserves a second mention.

MOWERS

If you have a lawn you need a mower. And unless you sensibly decide that it is crazy to acquire a noisy bit of machinery to cut a lawn the size of a face flannel when an old-fashioned push one will do, you will probably opt for an electric rotary mower. However, most men and other enthusiastic lawnists will hanker after or insist on the biggest mower possible (probably petrol, which is a very man-thing), and may even go for an old-fashioned cylinder mower that cuts really short and has a roller so that they can get 'stripes'. This is all very well if you have excellent grass and the site is very flat and you mow regularly.

The best type of mower for a lumpy lawn and wet grass is a rotary rather than a cylinder mower: one with a wheel at each corner, a whirring blade underneath and a grass collection box. There are all sorts on the market, in various sizes with all sorts of special features to make, it is claimed, your mowing life more pleasurable. You can get rotary mowers with tiny rollers on the back which will give you a bit of a stripy effect as long as you walk up and down your lawn as if you are your dad using a proper cylinder mower. I have always found, however, that for little lawns a kind of 'hoovering' action is easier to do, so the roller wasn't really significant.

There are some excellent battery-powered rotary mowers, which are more expensive than electric ones but mercifully quiet. It has to be said that the best petrol-powered rotary mowers, despite their noise and smelliness, are extremely robust. So for really big lawns and rough grass, a petrol-powered rotary mower will just about cope with anything you point it at. I had one of these once. Nicknamed The Snorter, it was a veritable off-roader with attitude, and I developed a great affection for it. But for me, now, in a smaller garden, my lithium-ion battery-powered mower, as light as a feather, wins hands down.

When you start measuring your garden in acres and parts thereof, it is probably time to acquire a sit-on mower. Since these should come under a general heading 'Boys' Toys', I would not dream of offering any opinions or advice, since I am sure they would be completely ignored.

SHEARS AND TRIMMERS

Ideally, you should have two kinds of shears: the long-handled type used for edging the lawn and a pair of ordinary hedge-cutting shears. If you have a really small lawn, you can just about get away with using an old pair of scissors for the lawn edge. The proper shears, however, the acquisition of which will not break the bank, make the job a lot quicker and save all that grovelling around. What you absolutely do not need is a half-moon lawn-edging tool. These you can borrow from someone just once a year if you really think it is necessary to tidy up your lawn edge. If you 'tidy up' more frequently than this, you will end up with an exceedingly small lawn.

If I had unlimited time, I would always cut a small hedge by hand. There is something therapeutic about the sound of shears and satisfying about the precision and the personal contact you make with the plants as you sculpt them. You need shears, anyway, for all sorts of small jobs around the garden, from the mid-season trimming back of messy perennials like catmint to tidying up odd corners of grass and 'haircut' pruning of small shrubs such as potentilla. As with any tool that you use with arms extended, unless you are built like a shot-putter, it is important to choose lightweight shears. And treat them well. Clean them and wipe them with WD-40 before you put them away after each session. The sap from any hedge pruning will soon build up into a sticky, rusty coating on the blades, and they will deteriorate fast.

Perhaps belonging in a category called 'Luxury Items', one-handed topiary shears should get a mention here. Personally I can't get on with those crissy-crossy-bladed things that seem to be so popular. So I use some Japanese-style Jakoti shears (actually mine are half the price of real Japanese ones, made in Greece and probably originally designed for shearing goats). They have eye-catching scarlet handles and a secateur-type spring. They are extremely useful for the speedy cutting-down of border perennials and grasses. (A useful tip: to avoid making a dreadful mess, tie grasses in a bundle before you cut them down.)

Power trimming

Urban and suburban hedge trimming with a petrol power tool is inevitably a very obtrusive activity, second only to petrol-shredding (see below) in its anti-social nature. The smell, noise and sheer weight of such machinery always stopped me acquiring one, even in my big-garden days, so I was all-electric (spending far too much precious hedge-trimming time, of course, mending severed cables...). However, as soon as the new generation of lightweight battery tools became available I ditched my electric trimmer in favour of a battery one of similar weight and power, and have never regretted it. Battery-powered trimmers are super-quiet and super-light, safe and manoeuvrable – and are surprisingly powerful.

SHREDDERS

Strictly speaking, all woody prunings and hedge trimmings should be snipped up into little pieces about 4cm (1½in) long before they are put in a compost heap so that they will rot down properly. This involves the most tedious waste of precious gardening time, and the job is particularly irksome if you often have a large quantity of prickly stuff like pyracantha or roses to process.

It was a great day for gardeners when they invented the shredder, and in particular the electric 'quiet' shredder, originally developed in response to stringent German noise-pollution regulations. These have wheels (thus can be stored easily in the garage or shed) and are a wonder to behold in action, virtually feeding themselves once you have introduced the material into their 'mouths', munching discreetly with barely a murmur on pieces of wood thicker than your thumb, reducing all manner of garden clippings and trimmings to about a quarter of their bulk.

The other bonus is that thus minced, garden waste takes far less time to compost and can therefore be returned to the soil in double-quick time to do the utmost good. Shredding is one of those low-brain-activity gardening jobs that can become almost addictive. I have found myself scouring the garden hunting for suitable material to shred, eyeing up likely branches of invasive trees and, on one occasion, even offering to shred the neighbour's prunings.

Petrol shredders? I am not even going to go there. If you really think your garden waste is too chubby for an electric shredder, then hire one. And make sure your neighbours are out when you use it.

Having said all this in praise of shredders, I should add the following. Most soft and sappy greenery does not strictly need to be shredded, and too much of it will tend to clog up even the best electric shredder. If I have a lot of greenery to compost (autumn border cut-downery, for example), I just lob it into one of my indispensable tip bags (see 'Useful odds and ends', below) and slash at it with my garden shears to make sure the toughest stems are cut up a bit.

Finally, the sort of mumsy advice you expect to find in all gardening books now. Despite the fact that all-singing, all-bleeping, instant cut-out safety mechanisms have now been built into the latest generation of shredders, you should always take care when using them, wear your stoutest gloves, put down your secateurs and never try to absent-mindedly push any stubborn bits into them using your hands (which won't fit, but your gloves can get caught up and give you a nasty scare). It should go without saying that this is not something that children should 'help' with, but I will say it anyway.

USEFUL ODDS AND ENDS

I am nearing the end of this book and I find myself wishing I did all the things that I advise everyone else to do. And perhaps regretting so many revelations that will surely diminish my 'gardening cred'. So, to cap it all, here are some scruffy items I find necessary and that form the useful chaos of my garden bits and bobs collection.

Plant labels and an indelible pen
Ordinary pencil wears off before your memory has time to take over (if you have one). I now favour black plastic labels and indelible silver pen. Very smart. As used in all the poshest of gardens.

A small hammer
It is simpler to acquire one especially for the garden. You also need a bag of galvanised staples and nails. You might also need a club hammer for banging all sorts of things into the ground.

A few plantclips
A cross between a clothes peg and the things you close food bags with – very useful for keeping shoots and branches of climbers out of your way while pruning.

An assortment of bamboo canes
When they get old and past it, I cut them up into short lengths to use as markers for 'invisible' plants such as newly planted bulbs, and as props for 'sticks-and-string' design modifications. Wooden kebab sticks (from supermarkets) are also useful as almost-invisible markers to show where you have planted seeds. Cats don't like the pointed ends...

A plastic measuring jug
This should have the words 'garden only' written on the side with the indelible silver pen.

A Sussex trug/a large bendy rubber bucket/trug with two handles/ wire basket with a handle/assorted tip bags
All of these are useful when weeding, and for carting things around when a barrow would be unnecessary.

A 1.25-litre (2-pint) pump-spray bottle with a green lid
I keep this one for insecticides and fungicides. Draw, in indelible pen,

a large picture of a greenfly on its back with its legs in the air, since it must never be confused with the next item.

A 1.25-litre (2-pint) pump-spray bottle with a red lid
Keep this one for weedkillers. Draw a lurid skull and crossbones on it. Nothing should be left to chance.

Old kitchen knives, forks and spoons
Keep these in a compartmented box, with other small items, such as labels and pens.

A green reinforced plastic sheet with handles at each corner
I call this The Drag. Self-explanatory and indispensable. Failing this, the absolutely biggest tip bag (from Bosmere) is useful.

And finally... one last essential – a light in the shed In my old garden, I had a proper shed, and I am sure it was untidy because I always found myself putting things away at dusk. In the end I installed a light. Oh what a difference. Now that my garage is my shed, the problem doesn't arise, but I try to be as organised as possible in a limited space shared with a car, a washing machine, freezer and umpteen pots of paint. I have found that the secret is hooks: many of them, at various heights and spaced at various intervals on the walls, so you can hang up everything that can be hung, to minimise floor clutter. Also I have a really high shelf for storing any garden nasties out of sight. The things I use daily – my secateurs and gloves and hand tools – reside in the house in a little rack by the back door, along with the wet slippers, of course.

DIRECTORY OF SUPPLIERS

Many of the products mentioned in the text are available from your local garden centre. If you can't find a stockist for a specific product, consult the list below.

Bosmere tip bag: various online stockists, including Amazon; or Google 'Bosmere tip bag' to find the best price

Bradleys leather anti-bramble gauntlets: order from www.bradleysthetannery.co.uk, 01746 766563

Felco secateurs: www.worldoffelco.co.uk, 0208 829 8850

Flexi-Tie: for stockists and mail-order suppliers: www.flexi-tie.co.uk, 01629 636945

Garden Mentor app for iPhone and Android phones: available from iTunes, or visit www.gardenmentorapp.com

Growmore: made by various manufacturers; if you can't get to a garden centre buy online – just Google 'Growmore'

Haws watering can: www.haws.co.uk; mail order 0121 420 2494

Jakoti shears: www.handshears.co.uk 01458 850066

Nu-Can watering can: www.conveniencecans.com

RHS Plant Finder: in book form is available from www.rhsshop.co.uk. Or access the information online via the RHS website www.rhs.org.uk/rhsplantfinder

Rootgrow mycorrhizal fungi: www.rootgrow.co.uk, 01795 411527

Roundup Weedkiller Gel: www.roundup-garden.com, 0845 190 1881

Sequestrene: www.lovethegarden.com for stockists

Slug Clear Liquid Concentrate: www.lovethegarden.com for stockists

Sneeboer hand tools: www.sneeboer.com for stockists or buy online from www.crocus.co.uk or www.harrodhorticultural.com

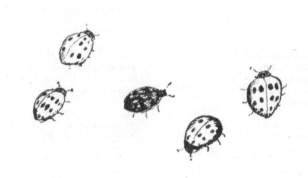

Index